e 1

First Grade
Writing Workshop

A Mentor Teacher's Guide
to Helping Young Learners Become Capable,
Confident Writers—and Meet the Common Core

Judy Lynch

New York · Toronto · London · Auckland · Sydney
Mexico City · New Delhi · Hong Kong · Buenos Aires

Teaching *Resources*

Dedication

To Kim Poppin, first grade teacher extraordinaire —
We started teaching first grade next door to each other over 13 years ago, when we discovered that we both "get" six-year-olds and we "get" each other. This year you shared your class with me and our lives and love of literacy intertwined even more. A toast to Mrs. Poppin!

To Principal Jim McLaughlin —
I always trust you to do what is best for kids (and you are my "go-to" guy when it's time to talk football).

To Donald Graves —
During your lifetime, you changed the lives of teachers and children around the world with process writing. Thank you from the bottom of my heart for changing me.

To the Placer Area Reading Council, affiliate of the California Reading Association and International Reading Association —
I grew up as a teacher and staff developer with all of you: Debi Pitta, Bev Ruby, Joyce Mucher, Sheila Simmons, Sandi Roullier, Linda Ashcraft, Getta Dolinsek, Cindy Tuisku, Tanya Cain, Carolsue Acres, Betsy Stenklyft, Kathy Goodwin, Joanne Ligamari, Beth Furdek, Joanne Devine, Jody Anderson, Taffy Maurer, Sherrill Renfro, Patty Calabrese, Muriel Secker, Katherine Beilby, Jenn Tverberg, Alisa DeLeo, Amy Nash, Frances Bigler and Deborah Schuman.

To my family who love and support my writing —
Mike, Michael, Emily and Madison, Shannon and Akif, and Kevin: You are my favorite team!

And special thanks to the best resources available —
Librarians Kathy Goodwin and Joanne Ligamari.

To E. B. White, author of *Charlotte's Web* —
"It is not often that someone comes along who is a true friend and a good writer. Charlotte was both." And so is every first grader we teach.

"In First Grade" by Donald Graves, used by permission of Betty Graves.

Editor: Eileen Judge
Supervising Editor: Mela Ottaiano
Acquiring Editor: Joanna Davis-Swing
Cover design: Jorge J. Namerow
Interior design: Melinda Belter
Cover photo by Doug Niva
Interior photos by Doug Niva, Judy Lynch, Carolyn Richards, and Kim Poppin
ISBN: 978-0-545-24005-5
Copyright © 2014 by Judy Lynch
All rights reserved.
Published by Scholastic Inc.
Printed in the U.S.A.

1 2 3 4 5 6 7 8 9 10   40   21 20 19 18 17 16 15 14

Contents

Introduction

In the summer of 1988, while attending the month-long California Literature Project, my new friend Bev Ruby handed me a book to read. She wanted me to try Writing Workshop with my first graders so, of course, the book was Donald Grave's *Writing: Teachers and Children at Work*. I read it that weekend and was hooked but filled with uncomfortable memories of my own writing in school. Writing was supposed to be "perfect" the first time we handed it in (there was no "work-shopping" of drafts when I was a kid), so little perfectionist Judy agonized over every word. As a result, I hated writing in school. In fact, I pretty much hated writing period until decades later when the personal computer came along with "delete" and "backspace" keys.

In his book, Dr. Graves described the "process approach" to writing, which I had never used in the classroom. In fact, as a student and as a teacher, there had been no "process" for me. Graves looked at how writers work and realized they could be anywhere in the five-stage process (prewriting; drafting; revising; editing; publishing). This process approach acknowledges that writers in the real world *don't* publish everything they write, and *don't* spell and punctuate perfectly in a first draft. Writers in the real world *do* plan their writing, and *do* get help from mentors and peers. If we want to teach students how to write, it only makes sense to teach what writers do. And so the process approach came to be adapted and applied to student writing as well.

Donald Graves also discussed the importance of students choosing their own topics for writing. The phrase "self-selected topics," made me chuckle when I thought of the story-starter wheel called "Title Twister" that I used in my early years of teaching: Before writing, one lucky student would dramatically spin the wheel, and we would see what exciting topic everyone would write on that day. "My life with the aliens," or "I looked in the mirror and I had turned into a . . ." or "My parents were pirates." Then, immediately, everyone was expected to write—without any discussion of the topic or brainstorming of any kind. And *choice?* I never stopped to consider that one of my students might have a new puppy at home or baby sister born the night before or perhaps even a new "window" in their mouth because of a lost tooth.

My eyes were opened wide by Donald Graves, and soon after by Lucy Calkins (*The Art of Teaching Writing*) and Jan Turbill (*No Better Way to Teach Writing*), and by many others over the years. But, at first, I wasn't sure where to start. Closing the door and turning to face 28 brand new first graders in the fall of 1988, I took a deep breath and just went for it. Everything I learned from those books about teaching writing was reinforced and shaped by my first graders that year and by the many experts in the field who have taught me since.

In 1990, the International Reading Association publication, *Reading Today,* had a small notice for a weeklong writing seminar with Donald Graves at St. Patrick's College in Dublin, Ireland. I called the college to find out how much of the seminar he would do. To my delight, they said Dr. Graves would be leading it in its entirety. This first grade teacher did a lot of extra tutoring to pay for the trip of a lifetime. What I learned that summer has influenced my writing workshops ever since. Moreover, Dr. Graves showed that he did not live in an ivory tower; and he proved that he knew first graders as well as we do by sharing his poem "In First Grade" with us.

In First Grade
by Donald Graves

In first grade
everything is edible:
soft, primary pencil wood
to run my teeth down
like corn on the cob.

Second course is paste
during reading while
Miss Jones' yellow eye
and green smile
catch me in mid-mastication
of a primary chairback
during story time.

Fresh erasers nipped off the end of a borrowed pencil
or brown art gum erasers
offered as hors d'oeuvres
from the art supply cabinet.

Then I reach for the fragrant
golden ends of Delores Gallo's
hair hanging over the back
of her chair and onto the books
on my desk.

At recess, rawhide webbings
in a baseball mitt, then green
crabgrass pulled just so
to gnaw white succulent stems
like salad at Sardi's.

Who needs warm milk
and graham crackers smelling
of the janitor's basement
at the Webster School
when we're already seven
courses in?

Teaching Writing: A Workout for Effective Instruction

Where are you when it comes to teaching writing to first graders? Comparing our expertise to exercise, are you still lacing up your sneakers or already running marathons? This book will lay the foundation for any of you who are in your first few years of teaching writing. It will also validate and support the writing instruction of you marathoners and everyone in between—and give you some practical twists and new ideas, too. The strategies, procedures, mini-lessons, and conference ideas, plus the teaching and management tips in *First Grade Writing Workshop* will help you take your writing instruction to new levels. In short, this book will give you the tools to get started or to review and refine your approach, and to build the stamina and enthusiasm (your students' and your own!) to keep it going for the long run.

How Does Writing Workshop Fit Into First Grade?

Language arts are a core component of the first grade curriculum; and learning to read is its cornerstone. Writing Workshop integrates well into our language arts curriculum, and writing does make better readers. "When individuals read, they go through a process that is similar to writing. The outcome of both reading and writing is that the individual constructs his or her own meaning. Given the similarities of these two processes, it is clear that they should be taught together. Research indicates that when reading and writing are taught together, students achieve better in both areas" (Tierney & Shanahan, page 246).

Furthermore, writing helps reinforce what students have read and learned. Research has shown that the reading strategy of retelling is an important way to assess, scaffold, and reinforce comprehension. Well, writing is like a high-powered retelling: it not only aids in comprehension, but has the additional benefit of helping develop vocabulary, phonics, and spelling skills, as well as craft skills like punctuation, style, and traits. Including Writing Workshop in your curriculum is like feeding your instruction a fitness shake. At right is a quick reference of the main terms and elements in a Writing Workshop program.

WRITING WORKSHOP WORKS BEST WHEN ALL SKILLS ARE TAUGHT IN THE CONTEXT OF SELF-SELECTED TOPICS.

Every school in every district has state-mandated standards in writing, spelling, grammar, and punctuation that students must learn. There is also usually state or school-district emphasis on the craft of writing itself, with understanding of and practice in various genres as the focus of different grade levels. Often these skills are taught as part of a standards-based basal reading series. These skills are definitely part of Writing Workshop with first graders. I like to supplement the writing skills introduced in our core basal with writing every day in workshop. The mini-lessons I use can echo what is introduced in a core program, but they also enable me to go in depth and use actual student work. "Canned" lessons in the basal are supplanted, and our work is brought to life with examples from my students each week. Worksheets are replaced with the authentic writing that happens daily in Writing Workshop. First graders are expected to take on the skills and craft of writing rather than fill out worksheets or do rote exercises. And again, I cannot stress enough how important choice is in motivating students and getting them to become fully invested in their writing and learning.

Writing Workshop Terms at a Glance

PREWRITE
Brainstorm.
Plan what I will write.

DRAFT
Write my ideas with words and sentences, even if they are not perfect.

REVISE
Reread my draft.
Add or take out words to make sense.
Fix my writing to make it better.

EDIT
Correct mistakes in my draft.
Correct for spelling, capitalization, and punctuation.

PUBLISH
Make a high-quality book of my finished writing.
Share my writing.

AUTHOR'S CHAIR
Read my writing to others.

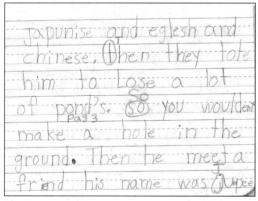

Bobby edits his own story for capitals and periods to prepare it for publication.

First Grade Writing Workshop © 2014 Judy Lynch • Scholastic Teaching Resources

CHOICE LETS FIRST GRADERS FIND THEIR VOICE.

Let's be honest, first grade writing is not the great American novel! It's writing that typically starts with "I like . . ." stories and can end with "bed to bed" stories, in which children tell the minutia of their day from sunrise to sunset in a list with few details. But occasionally you'll get a piece where you can "hear" their joy, sadness, excitement, or sense of humor. In my classroom, these stories are always shared in "Author's Chair." When this happens, students begin to see themselves as writers, and teachers quickly realize that letting students choose their topics gives them a voice.

DIFFERENTIATED WRITING INSTRUCTION IS A NATURAL FIT.

These young writers, indeed, have a voice, but every first grade teacher knows, they also come to the classroom with a range of skills and needs. With the workshop approach, I can incorporate state-mandated skills and Common Core Standards into my lessons, while at the same time differentiate my instruction based on students' needs. Every mini-lesson I offer is based on patterns I see when looking at student writing. Every conference with a first grader is individualized as I praise what they know and coach for what they need. Following each child, challenging when appropriate, and reteaching where needed are hallmarks of Writing Workshop. In this book, you will find ideas on how to do just that, and forms to keep track of it all.

WRITING WORKSHOP STRENGTHENS THE ENTIRE FIRST GRADE EXPERIENCE.

First grade teachers are busy all day with curriculum that is both dear to them and also mandated. For me, the curriculum I love integrates writing not only with reading but also with math, social studies, and science. I have found that I teach the mandated curriculum most effectively by having students write every day about topics they have chosen and that are dear to *their* hearts, such as new siblings, favorite activities, or family pets. And my first graders have been successful with this approach. Using Writing Workshop across the curriculum helps students think about, process, and reinforce all that they have learned.

Writing Workshop also dovetails with our

First grade writing can have voice.

I like roses. They are blooming. It is spring. We wear shorts and we wear short sleeves. The sun shines on the roses. Rainbows are coming out. I spy spring.

Sebastian and his new brother

> I Like being a Big brother. I have a litel sister and a new brother.
> I Help my Mom Take care of Them. My Mom Said I'm the Bes Big Brother.

Sebastian writes about being a big brother.

study of a full range of topics, themes, science, and social studies. Integrating writing across the curriculum each day actually creates the space for all that we have to pack in to teach first grade. Workshop mini-lessons can include modeled writing, shared writing, interactive writing, and student writing samples, using all the content studied during first grade.

After becoming familiar with my strategies for teaching writing to first graders, my hope is that you, too, will close the door, face your brand new first graders, and just go for it. So, let's get started; I will show you how.

Meeting the Common Core State Standards

The Common Core State Standards (CCSS) spell out the skills children are expected to master in writing from kindergarten through the end of high school. The idea behind the initiative is to uniformly boost student achievement across the country. If you are in a state that has adopted the CCSS, you will be relieved to know that Writing Workshop, with its process approach to writing, is a long-established format for meeting these standards. Here are the standards and some quick examples of Writing Workshop topics, mini-lesson ideas, and writing assignments you can use to help meet them. [Note: Standards 4, 9, and 10 start in higher grades but they are included below so that you can see where your first graders are headed.] Please visit http://www.corestandards.org.

Standard	Topics, Lesson Suggestions
TEXT TYPES AND PURPOSES	
W.1.1: Write opinion pieces in which [students] introduce the topic or name the book they are writing about, state an opinion, supply a reason for the opinion, and provide some sense of closure.	• Simple book report (This response to literature can be done in Writing Workshop as an individual choice or as a small-group assignment.) • Letter to the teacher, stating an opinion on where to go for the next field trip • Letter to the principal, proposing longer recess or new P.E. equipment • Letter to the president, governor, or mayor about an issue the students choose
W.1.2: Write informative/explanatory texts in which [students] name a topic, supply some facts about the topic, and provide some sense of closure.	• Simple reports or informational paragraphs on any science topic you study (for example: seasons, weather, water cycle, and life cycle of the egg, butterfly, or frog), or on any social studies topic you study (for example: family, Johnny Appleseed, Thanksgiving, holiday traditions around the world, presidents and other famous Americans)
W.1.3: Write narratives in which [students] recount two or more appropriately sequenced events, include some details regarding what happened, use temporal words to signal event order, and provide some sense of closure.	• Self-selected narratives; first graders love to write about themselves. Offer mini-lessons that teach them how to include words like *first, next, then,* and *finally* to provide sequence. (Examples of favorite topics: losing a tooth, taking a family vacation, playing a game at recess, and telling about a new baby or pet in the family.) • Field trip report. This could also work well as a small-group assignment, where students recall what happened on a field trip and use temporal words to sequence the events.

First Grade Writing Workshop © 2014 Judy Lynch • Scholastic Teaching Resources

PRODUCTION AND DISTRIBUTION OF WRITING

W.1.4: (Begins in grade 3) With guidance and support from adults, produce writing in which the development and organization are appropriate to task and purpose.	Note: Although this standard is not expected until Grade 3, the foundation for it begins long before then—and the 3rd grade teachers will thank you! Modeled writing in mini-lessons can show Beginning/Middle/End as we think aloud to retell a story or an event that happened at school. Many concrete examples provide development and organization.
W.1.5: With guidance and support from adults, focus on a topic, respond to questions and suggestions from peers, and add details to strengthen writing as needed.	• Mini-lessons that model how to choose and narrow topics • Mini-lessons that model how to add details • Teacher feedback during a conference, differentiated for each student • Opportunities for peer questions and feedback on a work in progress (for example: during Author's Chair, or in small-group or partner work)
W.1.6: With guidance and support from adults, [students] use a variety of digital tools to produce and publish writing, including in collaboration with peers.	• Teacher models how to publish a book on the computer by typing a student's work that is ready to publish. Gather the class around you and think aloud about the process. • Students publish a book on the computer with the help of an upper-grade buddy who does the typing but collaborates about the layout and font selection.

RESEARCH TO BUILD AND PRESENT KNOWLEDGE

W.1.7: Participate in shared research and writing projects (e.g., explore a number of "how-to" books on a given topic and use them to write a sequence of instructions)	• Write on favorite "how-to" topics (for example: build a snowman, play a recess game, make a gingerbread house or a snack, and take care of a baby)
W.1.8: With guidance and support from adults, recall information from experiences or gather information from provided sources to answer a question.	• Science lessons provide opportunities to gather information and put it in writing. • Group science or social studies projects model how to recall and use information to answer a question about the subject of study (for example: water cycle or simple machines, or the life/contributions of a famous person). • Some math problems provide opportunities to write answers to questions (for example: "How big is our pumpkin?").
W.1.9: (Begins in grade 4) Draw evidence from literary or informational texts to support analysis, reflection, and research.	Note: You can lay the essential foundation for this standard by thinking aloud while doing modeled writing. This writing can be done while reading aloud content area texts or in a mini-lesson for Writing Workshop.

RANGE OF WRITING

W.1.10: (Begins in grade 3) Write routinely over extended time frames (allowing time for research, reflection, and revision) and shorter time frames (a single sitting or a day or two) for a range of discipline-specific tasks, purposes, and audiences.	Note: In my opinion, this standard starts in first grade rather than third. Typically, from the first day of first grade, students write on a topic for a day or two or over extended periods of time. They learn about a variety of genres and purposes and have a ready audience for support and feedback.

CHAPTER 1

Writing Workshop Basics

Since Writing Workshop isn't a part of every first grade program—yet—some of you may not be familiar with what it entails. This chapter will cover the basics: the scheduling and implementation of your Writing Workshop and mini-lessons; materials and supplies (for example, writing journals and folders, forms and charts), and other resources; organization, record-keeping, and managements tips; format options for presenting the mini-lessons; and more. But first, it is important to start with the writing process itself.

Five Stages of the Writing Process

Donald Graves' process approach to writing highlights five stages of the writing process to mimic how real writers write. Writers plan their writing before they start (prewriting). They write many drafts (drafting). They might go back to review and improve the content and word choice (revising). They check for errors in capitalization, spelling, and punctuation (editing). And though a piece may seem finished, writers don't publish everything. They might set aside a piece and come back to it later. They get feedback from other writers and mentors, and then complete it (publishing). This same format works for my first graders. They write daily and can be anywhere in the five stages of the writing process. I model all five stages in mini-lessons and do one-to-one conferences to support each student wherever he or she is in the process. The craft and skills of writing are discussed, modeled, and practiced (as a class, in small groups, and in individual conferences) every day in the context of topics the students choose. I am their mentor, but so are the other first graders in the class (and all the parent helpers and upper-grade buddies I can train).

I remember Dr. Graves talking about misconceptions about the five stages in writing; teachers and basals tend to have the whole class follow the process lockstep: the class prewrites on Monday, drafts on Tuesday, revises on Wednesday, edits on Thursday, and the publishes all together every Friday. NO, NO, NO! Not only does this format ignore the natural writing process, but it is absolutely crazy to try to publish an entire class of first grade writers at the same time! On any given day, six-year-olds are at different stages of the writing process; Writing Workshop flows because I can meet students' needs right where they are.

Tip

To be honest, there is a lot going on in Writing Workshop: mini-lessons, writing, revising, center work, Author's Chair, conferences, etc. Managing it all is key to keeping it going—and keeping your sanity. I have developed a simple, easy-to-follow method to keep track of what's going on and where all my students are: a clipboard and a couple of handy forms (which I'll cover later in this chapter). That's it. Couldn't be simpler. I keep my clipboard with me at all times, and it keeps me organized.

5-STAGE Writing Process in First Grade

PREWRITE: Mini-lessons focus on students' needs and state standards. (Let children pick their own topic or choose one related to the curriculum you are teaching.)

DRAFT: The majority of first grade writing is in rough draft form. (Give children ample time to work on their drafts—but not too much time at first; they need to build stamina over time.)

REVISE: Revision "first grade style" usually happens when students respond to their teacher's nudging questions during an individual conference by adding to or clarifying their writing. (It can also happen as a result of partner work or peer suggestions/questions during "Author's Chair".)

EDIT: First graders can look for mistakes in spelling, capitals, and punctuation. (Note: At this grade, however, the final edit before publication is always done by the teacher or parent helpers.)

PUBLISH: The focus is on time spent writing, but we occasionally take rough drafts all the way to publication for each child.

The following are ways to implement your Writing Workshop lessons:

Format & Scheduling

Daily Format, 30–60 Minutes

I believe in the KISS method of teaching: *Keep It Simple, Sweetie!* So the daily format is this easy:

- Teacher does a mini-lesson.
- Students write.
- Teacher conferences with some students each day.
- A few students share their work (whether completed or in-progress).

Early in first grade, the total time spent writing, conferencing, and sharing is brief, but increases as the students build writing stamina and can focus for greater lengths of time. I like to do writing in the afternoon, because it gives me a chance to teach a mini-lesson or content first in the morning, but you can decide where it fits best in your schedule. Ideally, students should be writing five days a week, but the reality might be that you only have three days for Writing Workshop. If you can only manage three times a week, make sure the days are consecutive, say, Tuesday, Wednesday, and Thursday. Of course, other times in the day, students will likely write in response to small-group reading lessons and integrate writing with literature, science, social studies, and math—and that is a good thing. Remember, when it comes to writing, more is always better.

Below is a sample schedule with 30 and 60 minutes allotted for Writing Workshop each day.

Sample First Grade Writing Schedule

ACTIVITY	TIME BLOCKS	
FOCUS	30-MINUTE WORKSHOP	60-MINUTE WORKSHOP
Pre-writing/ Mini-lesson	5 minutes	10-15 minutes
Writing (students); 1:1 Conference (teacher/student)	20 minutes	30-40 minutes
Sharing/ Author's Chair	5 minutes	10-15 minutes

Materials & Supplies

When I started Writing Workshop with my first graders in 1988, I made simple journals using materials in the supply cabinet at school. Today is not much different. . .but now I get help making those journals. Experience has also taught me not to wait until August to get my materials and supplies in order: journals, pencils, crayons, folders, alphabet charts, word charts, and more. And in general, there is just so much to get ready before the start of the school year, you might want to get a head start on some things as soon as you can. There's a convenient list of suggested materials and supplies at the end of this chapter.

Journals

I like to start the school year with my writing and reading journals ready. August is busy enough setting up a classroom without the daunting task of stapling journals all by myself. So, I have learned to get them done *before school is out the previous year*! As school winds down in late May or early June, I get upper-grade students to help me start making journals for the next school year. Upper-grade teachers are usually more than willing to let a couple of capable students miss some of the room cleaning/DVD-watching that goes on during the last few days of school.

MAKING YOUR OWN

Making your own journals isn't complicated at all; you just staple pages together. I recommend the following materials: cardstock or heavy construction paper for the covers; unlined copy paper or paper with simple, clean lines for the interior pages; and a good stapler or two (for journal up to 20 pages, a regular stapler is fine; for journals with 20–30 pages, you'll need a heavy-duty stapler).

I like to start first grade with unlined paper so that students focus on composing the message rather than on writing on lines (a fine motor task that can take on a life of its own early in first grade). If your students are used to writing on lines, then go ahead and offer a choice of lined or unlined journals at the start of school.

Upper-grade helpers make journals at the end of the year that I will use when first grade starts in September.

PURCHASED JOURNALS

Depending on my budget, some years I have bought commercially made journals. My current favorite is the Mead Primary Journal K–2. This "Primary Writing Stage 3" journal has 100 sheets (200 usable pages front to back) and has blank-top paper with colored lines. When possible I buy them when back to school sales start and have even found them in my local grocery store with school supply displays. I transition students into lines when their first unlined journal is complete.

Writing Folders

During those same back to school sales, I buy inexpensive writing folders with inside pockets. I reinforce them with clear, wide packing tape when they start to come apart, but some students will need a replacement later in the year. The left side pocket holds high-frequency word and ABC charts. The right side pocket holds the writing journal. Right at the beginning of the year, I do procedural mini-lessons, and we practice how to:

- open the folder and take out materials.
- put the closed folder out of the way.
- carefully put materials back in the folder.

We practice this routine until it becomes a habit.

Resources to Support Writing

PENCIL SHARPENER

Busy first grade writers need sharp pencils. I finally bought the heavy duty electric one that can sharpen a pencil in a few seconds. I put former students to work who peek in and ask, "Do you need any help, Mrs. Lynch?" Sharpening pencils can also be one of the classroom jobs. Children should always have pencils at their desk, or have a good supply available at tables or supply areas.

ABC Chart

Aa	Bb	Cc	Dd	Ee
Ff	Gg	Hh	Ii	Jj
Kk	Ll	Mm	Nn	Oo
Pp	Qq	Rr	Ss	Tt
Uu	Vv	Ww	Xx	Yy
Zz				

Reproducible 1
126
First Grade Writing Workshop © 2014 Judy Lynch • Scholastic Teaching Resources

Teachers can insert the graphics that go with their own phonics/reading program into a blank ABC chart.

Tip

Thoroughly teaching five words a week will build mastery of the words students need for reading and for writing. Using the Word Wall as a reference is expected in Writing Workshop and throughout the day.

ALPHABET CHARTS

Our first grade team made an 8.5" x 11" chart to go along with our basal reading series. It matches the large alphabet strip above the white board and provides a link for reading, phonics, and writing. It can be confusing for first graders to have one style alphabet strip over the white board and another used in the reading program and yet another used in phonics, so it's a good idea to make them look consistent.

I photocopy the charts on white cardstock and put them in upright plastic holders (menu display holders found in office supply stores) on every table and on the reading table. I also make a copy for each student's writing folder.

HIGH-FREQUENCY WORD CHARTS

I like to use three different charts as the class and individuals are ready for them. I start with a review of 20 Kindergarten words, and later give them the 50 most-frequently-used words. Eventually I can transition to a chart with the 100 most-frequently-used words. I also provide children with a list of high-frequency irregular words that do not follow typical phonics pronunciations and thus are often misspelled by first graders.

CLASSROOM WORD WALL AS A REFERENCE

From the first day of first grade, I start building a word wall of high-frequency words. In those first weeks of school, I will also add students' pictures to the wall as an added reference for sounds. Our reading program has a bear to go with the letter

---

Review Words to Start the Year

a	and	at	can
dad	have	he	I
in	is	it	like
love	mom	of	see
she	the	to	you

Reproducible 2
First Grade Writing Workshop © 2014 Judy Lynch • Scholastic Teaching Resources
127

Review Words to Start the Year

---

50 High-Frequency Words

Aa	Bb	Cc	Dd	Ee
all and are	because by	can come	did do	each
Ff for friend from	Gg go	Hh have his her how here	Ii if into is	Jj
Kk know	Ll like little look love	Mm make may me more	Nn nice now	Oo or
Pp play	Qq	Rr	Ss said see she some	Tt the they this them
Uu	Vv	Ww who was what went when where	Xx	Yy Zz you

Reproducible 3
128
First Grade Writing Workshop © 2014 Judy Lynch • Scholastic Teaching Resources

50 High-Frequency Words

---

100 High-Frequency Words

Aa	Bb	Cc	Dd	Ee
a as all at an and by are	be because but by	come can come	dad day did do down	each eat
Ff family find first for friend	Gg get go good	Hh had here has him have his he how her	Ii if in is it its	Jj jump
Kk know	Ll like little look love	Mm make my man may me mom	Nn nice no not now	Oo of out on over one or other
Pp play put	Qq	Rr read	Ss said saw see she so some	Tt than they that this the to them too then two
Uu up us	Vv very	Ww was when we where went who were will what with	Xx	Yy Zz you

Reproducible 4
First Grade Writing Workshop © 2014 Judy Lynch • Scholastic Teaching Resources
129

100 High-Frequency Words

Irregular High-Frequency Words

the	of	a	to
you	was	are	they
from	have	one	what
were	there	your	their
said	do	many	some
would	other	into	two
could	been	who	people
only	water	very	words
where	through	any	another
come	work	does	put
different	again	old	great
should	give	something	thought
both	often	together	world
want			

These irregular words represent 53 of the 100 most frequent words. Adapted from Dr. John Shefelbine.

Reproducible 5
130
First Grade Writing Workshop © 2014 Judy Lynch • Scholastic Teaching Resources

Irregular High-Frequency Words

"b," but nothing makes the letter-sound relationship as concrete and memorable as the link from "b" and /b/ to *Bobby* and *Brian*.

Student pictures on the Word Wall; "B is for Bobby and Bryan."

WRITING WORKSHOP CLIPBOARD

"How do I keep track of everything?" was my first thought when starting Writing Workshop all those years ago. As teachers, we may be used to having the entire class be on the same page. However, giving six-year-olds topic choice and the ability to work at their own pace in the writing process could drive you crazy if you don't have a way to manage it all. Keeping track of where students are is made easy if you keep notes and forms together on your "Writing Workshop clipboard."

The form on my clipboard lets me keep track of two weeks at a glance. Because the space for each day is small, I use shorthand symbols to remember:

- who I have seen for a conference **(C)** each day
- how that student is doing

  C+ = the student is doing well

  C = the student is doing OK

  C− = I have concerns about this student

- when each student has shared in Author's Chair: ☆
- when each student asks a question of the student in Author's Chair: **?**
- when each student publishes: **P**

Below each day, I note what mini-lesson I did that day.

As you can see from the sample from a two-week span in November (see page 16), one simple form can contain quick notes that help me see at a glance how each student is doing, who needs help, and what help is needed. This information guides my conferences. Some conferences are just a quick check-in (for one minute or so) and others are a more involved chat. First graders also love to share their work, and the star on the chart let's me see who has shared so I can be fair to them all. When a student asks, "Can I share today?" I can check my clipboard to see when that child shared last. "Oh, you shared your writing last week on Tuesday. Let's give someone else a chance today." The star also

Writing Workshop Record

Name	Mon.	Tues.	Wed.	Thur.	Fri.	Mon.	Tues.	Wed.	Thur.	Fri.

Mini-Lessons:

C = Conference   C+ = Conference/student doing well   C− = Conference/concerns
P = Published   ? = Student asked a question   ☆ = Student shared in Author's Chair

Reproducible 6

Writing Workshop Record

Quick-and-easy clipboard form:
At the beginning of each school year, I create a simple organization method by writing my first graders' names down the left column of my "clipboard form," or Writing Workshop Record (Reproducible 6). I use first names only and put them in alphabetical order. (If you have more than one student with the same name, add first initial of their last names.) Then, I make 20 copies, which should last the whole school year.

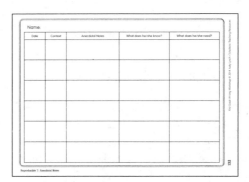

A sample of my clipboard for a two-week span in November.

helps me identify the shy ones and encourage them to share. I can also do a quick check of question marks (**?**) to note who has been asking questions of the students sharing in Author's Chair. This helps me make sure all students are participating. I realized some years ago that the same kids were asking all the questions and the rest were sitting on the rug kicking back and letting a few students do all the work.

For many years, this two-week form on my clipboard was all I used. I still use it throughout the year, but now I also use another form for longer anecdotal notes.

I keep these on the clipboard, too, and can add more detailed notes as needed. I also take home 1/4 of the student's folders each Friday to review and add notes and comments. That way, at least once a month I look at each child's writing in depth and over time. I found that I couldn't do this kind of in-depth review as much as I needed during Writing Workshop itself because of the pull of 20–28 first graders for my attention. The Anecdotal Notes form helps me accomplish this. At the end of each Friday, I collect the next 1/4 of student folders and mark my clipboard with a "**TH**" (Take Home) by their names. Then, each Monday, I conference first with those students whose folders I took home and studied. I find that I have more meaningful comments and questions when I do this.

Anecdotal Notes form

With Alana, for example (see page 17), I note how her writing evolves over time. In the space of a few weeks, she goes from disconnected letters to using spaces and writing two pages about her doctor visit in San Francisco. Her enthusiasm is sporadic until the end of October when her writing shows sustained effort on a more usual basis. I conference about what she knows and what she needs to do to advance as a writer. These notes also make accurate and easy-to-write comments for parent conferences or report cards.

When I take the writing folders home, I also review them to see if I am missing any trends in students' writing: same topic repeated for days; lack of effort day after day; more time spent on the illustration than the writing; emergence of voice; using periods when none were used before; sustained work over several days on a topic; etc. Before, when conferencing with a first grader, I tended to focus on the writing in front of them on the table. With this form and planned time for anecdotal notes, I can look at each student's writing in more depth and bring these observations to conferences.

Anecdotal Notes for Alana over several months

PROJECTION OPTIONS

Key to sharing writing in progress is a means to project it for all to see. Student work is the best example of the craft of writing, revision, and editing. I always ask permission to make a copy, but in general, first graders love to be featured as examples in our mini-lessons. Looking at student writing used to be done with an overhead projector, but most of us now use an interactive whiteboard or a document camera to project student work.

Gabby is at the overhead showing the class how she edits her writing.

Overhead Projector

If using an overhead, I start each year with a big box of blank transparencies, which are kept handy right by the projector. I also keep some in my mail cubby by the office for quick copying of student work.

Interactive Whiteboards

Interactive whiteboards are a great tool for shared writing. To use an interactive whiteboard to display student writing, you must have access to a scanner. Scan the work and save it on a computer to project onto the screen.

Document Camera

Document cameras come in many brands. I love them because there is no need to copy student work; just lay it under the "doc camera," and the image is transferred through an LCD projector onto an ordinary screen or whiteboard. Instant use of student work in full color is a great way to look at writing.

Materials & Supplies List

This list is intended to help you make choices for your classroom.
Adjust it to suit your needs.

JOURNALS
Purchased or Handmade (Covers Options: construction paper or cardstock; Paper
Options: lined or unlined)
Heavy Duty Stapler

WRITING TOOLS
Pencils
Colored Pencils, Colored Markers, Crayons
Pencil Sharpener
Pencil Jars (one labeled "sharp"; the other "dull")

WRITING FOLDERS (pocket folders)
Tape (Clear, wide tape to reinforce folder edges and make repairs as needed)
Pencils
Pencil Sharpener
Date Stamp
Heavy Duty Stapler
Sentence Strips
Scissors
Alphabet Charts
High-Frequency Word Charts

MINI-LESSON FORMAT OPTIONS
Chart Paper and Colored Markers
Document Camera
Interactive Whiteboard
Overhead Projector and Transparencies

CLIPBOARD FORMS
Writing Workshop Record Form
Anecdotal Notes Form

PUBLISHING
Book-Making Supply Tote
Making a Book Checklist
Extra Folders (for students making a book)
Cardstock for Covers
Colored Pencils, Markers, Crayons
Publishing Templates (for students and/or volunteers)
Student Photos (for About the Author pages)

LETTERS HOME
Prepare in advance any letters you will send home regarding:
Writing Workshop Volunteers * Publishing Guidelines * Help With Supplies

 First Grade Writing Workshop © 2014 Judy Lynch • Scholastic Teaching Resources

CHAPTER 2

Writing Workshop: Getting It Started

We looked at schedules and materials in the previous chapter. Now, it is time to open the door on the first day of first grade and get started.

Procedures, Mini-Lessons, Conferences

We have 180 days of school in my district. That means about 180 possible mini-lessons on writing each day! "NO WAY!" you say. "THAT JUST SOUNDS IMPOSSIBLE!" Well, just like life, the only way to make this possible is if we do it one day at a time. The Common Core Standards and my state's standards form a broad framework for my year's writing curriculum. But day in and day out, *this* class of first graders and *their* writing drive my mini-lessons. I certainly have some favorite mini-lessons that I've taught over the years, and I'll share them here with you, but there is no pre-determined day-by-day schedule. Each class of fresh-faced six-year-olds will get mini-lessons differentiated for their needs.

Procedures: Presenting the Mini-Lessons

No matter how I present a mini-lesson, foremost in my mind is what first graders need to know to get started in Writing Workshop. At the beginning of the year, I keep a copy of the "What First Grade Writers Need to Know to Get Started" chart (below) on my clipboard and at my desk, as a reminder before doing mini-lessons or conferences with my students. I recommend that you make an enlarged copy and keep it handy as a reference, or create your own on chart paper. You might also scan it to your computer and print copies as needed.

What First Grade Writers Need to Know to Get Started

- What we say can be written down.
- We can practice articulating words slowly to stretch and hear sounds so we can write them down—"rubber-band writing."
- Printed symbols are associated with sounds.
- We can record the sounds we hear in words.
- There is a one-to-one correspondence between spoken and written words (each spoken word = a written word).
- Words are made up of letters.
- Sentences are made up of words.
- We put a two-finger space between words to make them easy to read.
- Our writing moves from left to right with a return sweep—just like in books.
- We can add to the previous day's writing.

This broad guideline will be fine-tuned by what a particular class needs as evidenced by their early writing coming out of kindergarten. Carol Avery (...*And With a Light Touch*) reminded us many years ago that mini-lessons can come in a variety of formats. Whatever the content of your mini-lessons, the presentation is equally important. There are several different methods and modes for presenting a mini-lesson. Mixing up presentation modes keeps me from falling into a rut of perhaps just doing modeled writing every day—and keeps the students engaged and active. When students are engaged and share their writing, new voices are added. Following are my six favorite options for presentation of mini-lessons.

1. Teacher Think-Aloud With Modeled Writing

Writing in front of students can be done using chart paper, an overhead projector, an interactive whiteboard, or document camera. I take modeling to another level by thinking out loud about the process of composing, revising, organizing, editing, etc. Thinking aloud models the process of writing as it unfolds; it lets children see what writers do. This process may be obvious to us but is new to children who are now learning to write.

I plan a story in front of the class to model organization.

MATERIALS:

• Chart paper, overhead projector, interactive whiteboard, or document camera

• Pens

• Pointers for tracking print for the group to read

• Materials to bring attention to the details of the print:

  highlighter tape

  Wikki Stix®

  "windows" (I use fly swatters cut out to feature letters or words.)

  flashlight or laser pointer

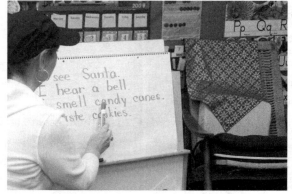

I use chart paper to model simple sentences using the five senses.

First Grade Writing Workshop © 2014 Judy Lynch • Scholastic Teaching Resources

OPPORTUNITIES FOR WRITING AND THINKING ALOUD:

- Morning Message
- Daily News
- Brainstorming sessions
- Notes to custodian, office, principal
- Invitations

- Thank-you notes
- Letters of apology
- Lists
- Special person stories or other stories
- Poems

A leprechaun wrote us an apology letter.

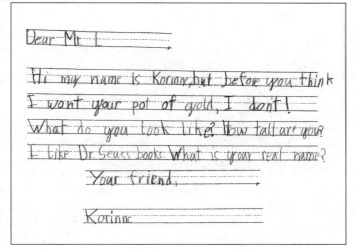

Korinne wrote a letter back to the leprechaun.

2. Interactive Writing

Interactive writing was developed by educators at The Ohio State University. Unlike shared writing, in which first graders compose messages and the teacher acts as scribe, interactive writing involves a sharing of the pen between teacher and students. It is a mini-lesson presentation option packed with skills for first grade writers. Details on how to use this strategy in early mini-lessons will be found later in this chapter.

3. Student Writing or Demonstration

My favorite mini-lessons usually come from student demonstrations and their writing. When conferencing, I often see a piece of writing that makes a good model to use in front of the class. I always ask a student's permission. I might say, "Can I make a copy for you to show everyone tomorrow? You can show everyone how to _____." Or, "Would you like some help or some comments on this from the class?" Students love to be showcased, even if it is to get help. For example, Emma showed the class how to circle spellings that look "strange." She knows how to spell "and" but noticed she had the "d" backwards. She showed the class how to check the alphabet chart to see the correct way to form a "d."

And Daesen didn't need me to make a copy of his journal. The class was gathered close on the rug and could admire the Table of Contents he made for his bear story. That very day, a few of his classmates tried the new technique he had demonstrated.

4. Act It Out

ROLE PLAY

Role-playing what to do and what *not* to do in Writing Workshop grabs the attention of those six-year-olds in front of me. Sometimes I do the acting, but frequently I get students to play along for dramatic effect. For example, I hate the noise pencil sharpeners make; they are loud and distracting. When I wanted to do a mini-lesson on sharpening pencils during class, I enlisted Lily to help me. I told her to start sharpening pencils when I started my lesson with the class on the rug. I began talking, and she got up and began grinding away on the pencil sharpener. I pretended not to notice, but the kids became annoyed by the noise. Finally I asked, "What's the problem?" They said all the things I would have: "I can't hear you." "Lily is making too much noise." "I can't concentrate." "Lily, do it later." So we came up with procedures for sharpening pencils at school:

- We will not sharpen during class.
- Helpers will sharpen pencils during recess or before/after school.
- We will use a holder for sharp pencils.
- We will use a holder for dull pencils.

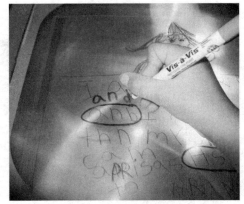

Emma demonstrates editing for spelling on the overhead projector.

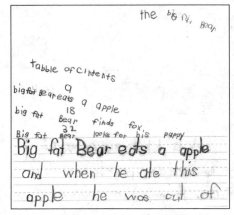

Daesan shows the Table of Contents he created to write his first "chapter book."

The Big Fat Bear
Table of Contents
Big Fat Bear Eats an Apple   9
Big Fat Bear Finds Fox   18
Big Fat Bear Looks for His Pappy   32

Lily role plays what not to do.

Every teacher knows that appropriate procedures and proper behavior are essential for teaching and learning to take place. I could have announced this procedure and "my rules for sharpening pencils" the first day of school. Instead, my first graders became part of the solution to a noisy problem that drives me crazy during lessons throughout the school day. This has twofold rewards: 1) When students are involved in the process, they are more likely to remember and feel accountable for the rules; and 2) When they watched me create the pencil-bin labels, they also saw that writing has some very practical purposes.

SPOTLIGHT

This strategy serves a variety of "acting it out" mini-lessons. I use it to demonstrate with a child or small group of children while the rest of the class gathers close by to listen in and watch. Spotlight is sometimes called the "fishbowl" because the class is gathered around the teacher, observing a lesson quietly.

A brief mini-lesson spotlights a small group, but the rest of the class is nearby to listen in.

Small-Group Spotlight

Landon, Bobby, and Jonathon are at a table with me and the rest of the class is on the rug nearby. I allow the students to be on their knees so they can see what we are doing and hear how I do a small-group conference. The class listens in as I model how to use periods in their stories rather than the word *and* over and over and over. I also talk with those on the rug about what they will do at their seats when I work with a group like this. The rest of the class is sent to write at their seats and show that they can be independent and not interrupt or distract my small group.

1–Student Spotlight

Spotlight can also be a great method to show a short whole-class mini-lesson in action by focusing the attention on one student—and encouraging everyone to eavesdrop.

When teaching a strategy, I may begin with a whole-class mini-lesson, for instance with me modeling how to spell a word. I might start out saying the word slowly and stretching the sounds in front of the entire group. I call this "rubber-band writing," and I stretch out an imaginary rubber band as I stretch out the word. First graders practice in front of me, but I want to reinforce that they need to use this strategy on their own when they try to spell words in their journals.

Spotlighting rubber-band writing with one student, Alana.

When the children go back to their seats, I sit in the middle of the class with one student, Alana, but I ask the class to watch and listen. The class hears us talk about her trip to the mall to get a new dress for church. (Note that Alana is writing about a topic of interest to her.) When she needs to spell "shopping," Alana shows me that she knows how to do rubber-band writing, stretching and recording the sounds one by one. (See page 113 for more on rubber-band writing.) We will use this strategy throughout the year to spell longer words that are not on our word wall. As a realist, I know that there will be many more mini-lessons and student conferences to reinforce this spelling strategy.

"Longer, Better Stories" list from Carol Davis "

5. Make a List

I like the idea of making an ongoing list with students. Each topic on the list can be a mini-lesson but usually represents a series of topics generated over time. I got the idea from Carol Davis, one of those magical first grade teachers. (Don't you get your best ideas when walking through the first grade class next door?)

Each part that was added to Carol's first graders' list of "Longer, Better Stories" was the foundation of many lessons.

However, first graders can't write longer stories just because a teacher puts "Details = tell more" on a chart. The same was true of the list my own class created for writing longer stories this year.

First graders can't make better word choices just because I put "Describe" on our chart. But this was the reference as I wove many mini-lessons into our Writing Workshop on how to use size, shape, colors, and the five senses to craft better stories. Our list was posted in the classroom to serve as a reminder about crafting good stories.

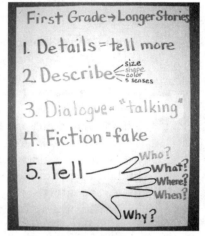

Our List: First Grade→ Longer Stories

6. Organizing Writing With Graphics

Graphic organizers lend themselves to the writing process—whether brainstorming ideas and details or organizing them. Mini-lessons using a variety of graphic organizers make the planning and writing process visually clear. My first graders can refer to the organizer while they write, helping them as they choose a new topic, respond to literature, write a report, or expand on a topic, among other writing options.

CHOOSE A NEW TOPIC

The first day of school and throughout the school year, we will brainstorm and chart topics. (For more on choosing topics and using topic charts, see pages 30 and 65.)

Brainstorming topics

RESPOND TO LITERATURE

For Dr. Seuss' birthday, we read and charted several of his books. The graphic organizer (see Reproducible 8) was useful to compare problems, solutions, and the author's messages.

Literature Comparison chart

Title	Characters	Problem	Solution	Author's message
Horton Hatches the Egg	Horton Mayzie baby elephant bird hunters	The bird didn't come back. Horton wouldn't get off the egg	The egg hatched.	You have to do your own work to get what you need.
Marvin K. Mooney will you Go!	Marvin K. Mooney	Marvin K Mooney would not leave.	He leaves.	When you are ask to do something, you should do it.
THE CAT IN THE HAT	Sally Conrad The Cat The Fish Thing One Thing Two	Thing One and Thing Two are making a mess.	To clean up the mess.	Do not let strangers in your house.

Celebrating Dr. Seuss created a great opportunity to analyze and write responses to literature.

Tip

Enlarge Reproducible 8 to make a chart like the one at left, which can be laminated and reused to compare other texts at other times. Book covers can be scanned, or you can take a digital picture, print it out, and attach it with Velcro.

WRITE AN INFORMATIVE REPORT

First graders love to bring "treasures" to school and tell about them. These occasions make wonderful opportunities to teach about descriptive writing. We brainstorm topic-related words on a group chart and then post the words close to the display area in our classroom. Why not turn "Show and Tell" into "Writing With Realia"?

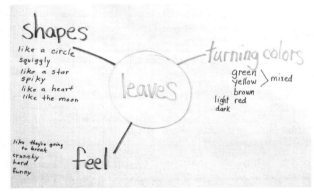

We brainstormed all about "Fall Leaves"...

...then used the graphic organizer and artifacts to write about them.

EXPAND ON A TOPIC

The Helping Hand organizer starts as a mini-lesson on how to revise a topic by asking *who, what, where, when,* and *why* questions about our writing. It evolves into a tool for one-on-one conferencing and a reference point for asking questions of a writer during Author's Chair. (See Chapter 3 for more on Author's Chair.)

Create your own Helping Hand organizer by tracing your hand and making enlarged photocopies or by projecting on a whiteboard or overhead.

The First Five Days of Writing Workshop

The early days of Writing Workshop are a blend of modeling how a writer gets ideas down in print and such practical matters as how students should take out and put away their folders. I need to cover both, so I do both during the first several lessons in first grade. Later mini-lessons will focus entirely on procedures, or skills, or the craft of writing. Here are those crucial early mini-lessons that are doubled up in the first days of Writing Workshop:

	PROCEDURES	CRAFT
Day 1	Folders/Journals	Choosing topics
Day 2	Dating your work	New story or Continue?
Day 3	Using the Topic Chart	No such thing as "done"
Day 4	Using an ABC Chart	What we say can be written
Day 5	Quick sharing	Matching words to pictures

"But how will I manage double lessons with a class of wiggly first graders?" you may well ask.

Every first grade teacher knows that the first week is tough on students who were kindergartners mere weeks ago. Lessons need to be short and focused to hold their limited attention. We need to be prepared, or they will bury us with those never-ending questions. . . "When do we eat?" or "When do we go home?"

Here's how I manage it in my class. We have our first writing lessons after lunch each day, so I do all my procedural mini-lessons *before we go to lunch.* The procedural lessons listed above fit perfectly into the 10 minutes before lunch at the beginning of the school year. *After lunch,* I can focus on the craft of being a writer. From the first day of first grade, I make a point to think aloud about being a writer. I let the class see and hear my thought process about taking care of my writing folder and choosing a topic.

Day 1

PROCEDURE: Folders/Journals

With great drama, I show the class my writing folder and talk about how I will take care of it this year. I model, and they practice the following procedures:

- I take out my folder (from my desk or a tub on the group table).

- I take the journal out of the folder.

- I close the folder and place it at the top of the writing area, out of the way.

- I open the folder and carefully put the journal back in the right pocket.

While at desks or tables, students practice taking out their writing folders, taking out the journals, and putting them back without bending the journal pages. We practice the procedure several times until it is done quietly and quickly. Now it is time for the students to go to lunch, but they should know what to do with their folders when we come back.

CRAFT: Choosing Topics

After lunch, it is time to start our main block of writing. Students are seated in front of me on the rug. I begin by letting them know what we will be doing each day at this time. "I want you to know that we will be writing every day, and writers are always thinking about what they might write. I know in kindergarten you loved to share what was happening with your family, friends, and at school. Now, we will write those things down and even make some stories into books."

Brainstorming

First, I tell students that they will need to think of something they want to write about, and that I am going to think of something, too. I model brainstorming three ideas I might write about this day (from Nancie Atwell's *In the Middle*). Thinking out loud makes this process visible for beginning writers. "I can write about the birds in my backyard—they must be mad at me because I didn't have time to fill their feeders before rushing to school this morning. *Or,* I could write about my party. Mrs. Poppin came and Mr. McLaughlin our principal did, too. Mr. Lynch barbecued, and everyone ate a lot of food. *Or,* I can write about my son's football team in Illinois . . . they started practice on Saturday."

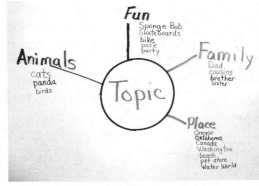

Our Topic Chart on the first day of school

I turn to a chart with a blank circle in the middle. I write the word "Topic" in the middle and announce that topics are things we enjoy writing about. We fill in ideas for topics together. *Family, Animals, Fun,* and *Place* are some of the categories I add as they brainstorm about family members, popular and unusual animals, places they have lived in or visited, and fun—from skateboarding to Sponge Bob.

How to choose from all the ideas?

I think out loud about narrowing my choices to just one: "I may write about the birds later. I better not write about my son's football team because I don't know enough since I'm not there. So, I think I'll write about my party." Notice, I follow the Donald Graves model and dismiss a topic because I don't know enough about it to write much. Early on,

I want students to choose a topic about which they are bubbling over with things to tell. The process of getting *all* they know down in print will take most of the school year, but having a topic worth the effort is the start.

"What are you going to write about today?" I ask. One boy says "skateboarding," and then I ask how many others want to write about that, too. I want to establish that they can share topics because each story would be different. Each child commits to a topic. They indicate they are ready to share their topic by giving a "thumbs up." This process takes time but pays off because they are committed to what they will write.

"Thumbs up" shows we know what to write about.

Before students leave the rug, I model how to take the topic I selected from the chart and put it on the top of the first page in my journal—like a heading. Now comes the important part—we are all going to write! I will write for a few minutes on paper (so that I have a piece to share the next day on the projector). Then I am up and about to conference with as many writers as possible. We only write for 10–15 minutes at the start of the year but will build stamina soon.

BRIEF CONFERENCES

Quick conferences are a great way to encourage details even with early writing. "What color is your new kitten?" "Where did you go skateboarding?" Wherever I can, I write what they read to me from their page in small cursive, and in pencil, at the bottom of their journal page. I do this unobtrusively but use it later so I can analyze what letter/sound matches they have mastered and what they need to learn. For students who have "readable" sound/letter matches, I don't do this. I take notes on my clipboard during the conference, and again after school when I look at their first day's samples.

Alana writes a few words she knows and sound spells "sister."

Oliver (an ELL) copies "beach" from the topic chart, adds words he knows, and sound spells others.

Jonathon writes an impressive full page with details and organization about his family's plane trip to Canada.

Alana writes, "Sister I love you."

"Beach I found hole I play"

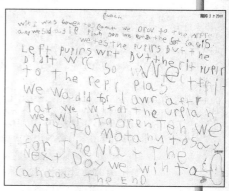

Jonathon's account of his plane trip to Canada

The first day of first grade Writing Workshop shows there is a range of skills—from copying words randomly from the topic chart, to writing strings of letters, to writing a pattern like "*I love...*," to writing one, two, or more sentences and using details on a full page account of a summer trip. We have our work cut out for us! But that is the joy of Writing Workshop with first graders—I can take them where they are and move them along from there. I will tailor mini-lessons and conferences based on *this* class—*this* week and throughout *this* year.

In this first week of school, there is no formal Author's Chair for sharing. To close out our session, I want to give feedback to as many students as possible, so I quickly move around the room asking, "What did you write?" When they announce their topic and tell what they've written, I give comments to encourage elaboration: *What else did your family do at the beach? What does your big sister look like? Can you describe her in words tomorrow? Where does your grandma live?* This quick sharing lets everyone shine and gives young writers the simple feedback they need.

STOP SIGNAL

Now, I give the signal to stop, a procedure we learned in the morning during math. I ring a chime, and students know to immediately put down their pencil and raise both hands up by their shoulders. Most teachers have a signal to get kids to stop what they are doing and "listen up." I keep a small wind chime at the front of the room that I use and say, "Stop, look, and listen."

Our "Stop, Look & Listen" procedure: When the chime rings, Gabby drops her pencil, raises both hands by her shoulders, and quietly looks at me.

With nothing in their hands and their eyes on me, I have their full attention and can give the next direction. Today, when I give the stop signal, I also give them good news: "Don't worry if you are not finished. We will write every day, and you can write more tomorrow. Writers usually don't finish everything in one day."

Before lunch, we practiced putting our journals away in our folders, so when I give the signal, I expect this procedure to be pretty much in place. And yes, we will practice this again and again if it gets sloppy or noisy later in the year!

Day 2

PROCEDURE: Dating Your Work

I want the work dated because this allows portfolio evaluation of students' writing growth over time. My goal is that they will write the month and day quickly by themselves in the top left corner of the page. The reality is that this procedure will take some intermediary steps.

Early Steps:

For the first few weeks of school, I use two date stamps that I prepare each morning. On the second day of school, my pre-lunch procedure is on how to help date students' work. With two helpers I have chosen, I model and think out loud about how to use the date stamps:

> • Date the top left corner of the page.
> • Stamp the date only once.
> • No talking while working.

Next, the class watches the helpers move quietly around the class for a minute or two. Then, I call on two more helpers to show what they have learned. For the first few weeks of school, students rotate helping date-stamp the journal pages.

Misty wrote the date by herself!

Later Steps

As soon as I have volunteer parents or older students in the class, I train them to write the date at the top of the page the moment they start working with a student. Since the start of school, the date appears on the whiteboard each morning in two forms: 9/10/13 and September 10, 2013. The helper writes the month and day in quick numerical (9/10) and calls attention to it. Gradually more and more students notice and copy this modeling.

Final Steps

After the first month of school, I announce that we will all write the date quickly by ourselves in the short numerical form (month/day). As I circulate doing conferences, I draw a star by the date of everyone who did this without a reminder. Isn't it amazing what first graders will do for a star?

CRAFT: New Story or Continue?

The first day, I purposely did not finish the story that I wrote on an overhead transparency. I intended to make it a cliffhanger with so little detail they will beg for more. It is important to share it and ask, "Have I finished my story? Have I told everything there is to tell?" I share what I wrote the day before on the projector: *I had a party*. I ask the class to shake their heads quietly yes or no—"Did I tell *everything* about my party?" Of course, they shake their heads "no." I want to model how to add to a story— so this first topic is one where it is obvious that it is not finished.

Continuing Work

I model how to put the date where I left off the day before. Rather than at the top, it can be to the left of where the writing stopped. First graders like the idea of showing off how many days they wrote on a topic. I ask, "Who else has more to write?" I remind them where the date will go on their paper and send them off to add details to their writing.

New Story

There will be a few writers who feel they told *everything* the day before. We look at the topic chart again, and they each choose something new to write about today. I remind them to put the topic at the top as a title and that their date-stamp will go on top left, too. With a commitment to the new topic fresh in their minds, off they go to write with the rest of the class.

Day 3

PROCEDURE: Using the Topic Chart

Before they go to lunch on the third day of school, I do a short mini-lesson to remind them how to choose another topic. We can add to the topic chart, but for now my main focus is using the chart we have. We practice reading the ideas under each main heading and embellish them a bit. I ask, "Is Bobby the only one who can write about his grandma?" "Is Alyssa the only one who can write about a dog?" We talk about how each of us would make these topics our own. Now, we do a quick review of writing the topic as a heading at the top of the journal page. I invite four students to come up with their journal and show everyone how to write the heading at the top—without talking to each other.

CRAFT: No such thing as "done"

Every first grade teacher dreads hearing the words, "I'm done." We always need a contingency plan for those "fast finishers." During reading and math, we have activities they can do that will reinforce their learning—and make sure they don't interrupt our instruction. But what about during Writing Workshop? No problem! My next mini-lesson might be titled, "There is no such thing as done!" I model writing a

> - Write more.
> - Draw a picture.
> - Pick something new from the topic chart and write about it.

few simple sentences in my journal. Then I announce, "I'm done" and proceed to close my journal and sit there looking bored. Finally I ask, "What can I do when I am done?" The class has lots of ideas, so we make a chart:

Hmmm…these are the very same suggestions I would have told them. But my dramatic little demonstration is more effective, plus they bought into the idea that when *we* create a chart together, *we* can add to it later. I close this mini-lesson by telling students about hearing Newbery Award-winning author Madeleine L'Engle speak. She told the audience that she waited a long time before *Wrinkle in Time* was accepted for publication. But while she was waiting, she worked on it to make it better, and she started other projects. She didn't just sit there and say, "I'm done!"

Day 4

PROCEDURE: Using an ABC Chart

I attend to spelling if it comes up the first few days of first grade. As I buzz around the room checking in with as many students as I can, I encourage sounding out unknown words by saying them slowly. The first one who says "How do you spell…?" gets encouraged—aloud, so all can benefit—to stretch the word slowly like a rubber band and put down all the letters he or she hears. I never spell for students on a rough draft or they will never apply their emerging phonetic knowledge; they won't learn to say words slowly and write the letters they hear. Instead, they will always depend on me, or another adult, to be their spelling source.

When trying to spell a word, the main thing I want students to do at this point is use an ABC chart to sound out words and make a link to our first grade phonics instruction. I model this for them, and then give each one a small version of the ABC chart (Reproducible 1) to keep in their folder.

I try to make sure students' individual charts match the ones posted around the room.

In addition to the individual ABC chart, I also remind students of the 20 high-frequency words from kindergarten that we are reviewing with the Word Wall (Reproducible 2, "Review Words to Start the Year"). Some students use the chart in their writing after lunch and are publicly praised. This praise gets the attention of others who realize, "Oh, I'm supposed to be doing something with this thing, too." In conferences, I use the chart and have them stretch the word they are trying to spell. We pretend we are slowly pulling a rubber band as we stretch the sounds in the word and record them in order.

CRAFT: What we say can be written

After lunch, I use this 4th-day mini-lesson to model how to get the words from our mouth down on paper. I have talked to Landon ahead of time so he will come up front and ask me, "Mrs. Lynch, what do you like to do for fun?" I reply, "I like to swim. Shall I write about that?"

I model writing my swimming story in front of them. As I model, we do the following:

1. Count the words I say on our fingers: "I like to swim." = 4 words

2. Spread our four fingers, and I tell them to notice the spaces between their fingers; these are like the spaces between words when we write.

3. Use the high-frequency word chart (that they each have) to write the first three words on chart paper (*I like to...*)

4. Use the ABC chart to stretch the sounds in "swim" with rubber-band writing. (See page 113 for more on modeling this important strategy.)

5. I choose another color pen to write the second sentence (*I can jump in the pool.*); this will emphasize they are two different ideas: (#1 *I like to swim*, #2: *I can jump in the pool*).

My conferences on this day will emphasize that students:

Say their sentence.

Repeat the sentence as we put each word on a finger.

Count the number of words they will write as they repeat it again.

Using the ABC chart to find letters to match sounds

Counting the words in "I like to swim" on our fingers.

Two sentences are finished as I model how to get words from my mouth to the page.

Day 5

PROCEDURE: Quick Sharing

Before lunch on the fifth day, I will model a quick procedure we can use during the first few weeks of school for sharing our work. This is an easy solution until I am ready to take the time and energy to teach the procedures for sitting on the rug for a more formal Author's Chair. This quick showcase of students' work involves bringing six to seven students up to the front at the end of writing. Here's how it goes:

Seven proud first graders Quick Share in front of the room.

1. Ring the chime for *Stop, Look & Listen.*

2. Announce those students who will be coming up front and note their names on my clipboard (adding a star by those names). Different students come up each day after this.

3. All other students put folders away and fold their hands on their table.

4. One at a time, each student shares his or her topic and writing, and gets brief feedback from me and the class.

CRAFT: Matching Words to Pictures

First grade pictures at the top of their paper can be penciled stick figures or elaborate crayon masterpieces. The picture gives them another creative outlet for telling their story. Early in first grade, most of the effort can go into the picture. I like to make the connection between the text and the illustration right away, so after lunch I do the following:

1. I draw an elaborate crayon picture of my house with trees, flowers, and my red car in front. (Only six-year-olds think my feeble attempt is just wonderful!)

2. I write in pencil underneath: "This is my house. I like my house."

3. Then I ask: "Do my words match the detail in my picture? What did I leave out? Let's make a list of what you see in my picture but don't hear in my words." (You might need to pry this out with questions.) Here's what the list might look like:
   - color of the house
   - size of the house
   - trees with green leaves and brown trunks
   - flowers that are pink and purple
   - red car

4. I tell students I will be looking to see who uses words to describe their whole picture when we conference. Those who do will get to share at the end. An opportunity to showcase their work is always a big "carrot" to encourage students to try something new.

Procedures: The First Six Weeks

Procedures make Writing Workshop run smoothly. I know I need to do a procedural mini-lesson when something is driving me crazy (*noisy pencil sharpening, students not listening when someone is sharing, students asking me to spell everything for them*, etc.). Below are some mini-lessons I do to keep Writing Workshop going smoothly during the first weeks of first grade.

GROUP TIME ON THE RUG
- entering the room after recess
- how to come to the rug
- how we sit
- where we sit
- active listening
- how to go to our seats

SEAT TIME
- getting right to work
- What does the room look like when we write?
- What does the room sound like when we write?
- working with minor distractions
- how to get help
- helping others when you can, and how to do it quietly
- clean up

SUPPLIES
- where they are kept
- pencils
  sharpening pencils
  holding the pencil
  using the eraser
  where to find extra erasers
  where to find a new pencil
- crayons
  when to use them
  how to take them out and return to the box
  peeling back the paper
  where extra crayons are kept to replace broken crayons
- folders
  how to open
  keeping journal and charts organized
  putting materials back in folder
- using ABC charts
- using high-frequency word lists

First Grade Writing Workshop © 2014 Judy Lynch • Scholastic Teaching Resources

Mini-Lessons: The First Six Weeks

"What do my students need now?" is always a valid question because they need everything! There is no such thing as a lockstep series of writing lessons because we must follow *this* class. My driving questions, as taught to me all those years ago by Donald Graves, are *What do they know?* and *What do they need?* Of course, there are common patterns first grade teachers see typically at the beginning of the year. For example, we often see strings of letters squished together that may or may not match the sounds and words they represent. Or they may not understand what makes a sentence. Still others may be ELLs. Here are some lessons to deal with these wide-ranging, early writing needs. The "What First Grade Writers Need to Know to Get Started" chart (see page 19), is also a good resource for these early mini-lessons.

Learning to Write With Spaces

Why do young writers smush everything together when they write? For me, the answer goes back to what they bring to school: oral language. When we talk, no matter what language we speak at home, it is a stream of speech sounds. This awareness of sounds is the foundation for Phonemic Awareness. Six-year-olds have heard this wave of sounds that doesn't clearly separate words. The fact is: *we don't talk with spaces!* The words we hear in conversation blend together, often the last syllable of a word sounds like it is part of the first syllable of the next word we say. But when they come to school, we give them books with spaces between words and simply expect them to know there are spaces between the words they write. "Spaces" are a convention of print that needs to be taught to emergent writers.

First graders first have to *get* that the words that we say can be written. And then they need to learn how to properly put those words on paper. To model the concept of spaces, I like to slow the whole process down with a mini-lesson:

"SAY IT, WRITE IT"

1. *Say a few words.*
   I ask Landon to come to the front of the room and open his journal. Conversationally, I say, "Look around the classroom and tell us something you see." He looks up, points to the flag, and says, "I see the flag."

2. *Everyone repeats the sentence.*
   "Did you all hear what Landon said? Everyone say it again slowly, and let's count the words on our fingers."
   All: "I see the flag." (4 fingers = 4 words)

3. *Write a few words.*
   With everyone watching, Landon says each word as he writes it. The whole class says each word with him and reminds him to put a two-finger space after each word. In these early weeks, we all spread our fingers out to remember the spaces kinesthetically.

4. *Show the words.*
   Landon proudly shows his sentence with words and spaces.

5. *The whole class practices "Say It, Write It."* Returning to their seats, partners use the *I see a/the _____.* frame to practice the strategy with "two-finger" spaces. I roam the room praising by name those students using spaces for their own sentence. I encourage further writing by announcing that if they want to tell something else that they see, they can put a period and start their new sentence with a capital. (Many lessons will be done over the year to reinforce that a sentence tells one thing, starts with a capital, and ends with a period; this is just the beginning.)

Landon says four words and writes four words (I see the flag).

Using Arm Spelling and an Alphabet Chart for Short Words

One of the first mini-lessons was to pass out the ABC Chart that goes in their folder. I model "rubber-band writing" at that point and suggest you model this strategy early in the year. (See pages 23 and 113 for more on "rubber-band writing.") Now it is time to show another spelling strategy for short words with guided student practice.

Tabitha spells "frog" by touching down her arm for each sound.

1. *Bring charts to the rug area*

    Before going to lunch, I have the class take out their writing folders, open them, and take out their ABC chart. When we come back later, they bring their charts to the rug area.

2. *Model "arm spelling" for short words*

    I remind the students that I had showed them rubber-band writing and that it works really well for sounding out long words. Now I'm going to show them another spelling strategy that works especially well with shorter words: "arm spelling." Then I show students that we can spell short words, like *frog,* on our arm. "Watch me spell *frog* by starting at my shoulder and touching down my arm for each sound: /f/ /r/ /o/ /g/. Now you try it."
    Next, I'll look at my chart to match the sounds I hear to the letters I see: f-r-o-g. Then, I tell students, "Get your eyes ready to find the letters on your chart while we touch our arms and spell *frog* slowly."

3. *Take turns saying and sounding out words to practice with the ABC chart.*

    Five students will be called on to give us words to practice arm spelling with the charts.

Note that at the beginning of first grade, all words seem long. Eventually, we will distinguish between long and short words, and we will use rubber-band writing for sounding out long words, like *dinosaur*. At this point, however, I specifically identify a word as "long" or "short." This helps students learn to distinguish between them, and decide on their own which spelling strategy to use.

I choose the first student and ask him or her to say a short name of an animal for us to practice sounding out and finding the sounds on our ABC chart. The whole class touches their shoulder and down their arm for each sound in this word, then we repeat with the chart. Practice the procedure with four more students picking words to sound out and spell using the chart.

4. *Allow time for guided practice.*

   Back at their seats, it is time for students to write. I remind them that I will be looking for those who are using arm spelling to hear sounds and their ABC charts to match letters to the sounds so they can write the words. Students who try it will have a chance to showcase their words for sharing at the end.

Of course, ALL first graders want a turn and will beg you to choose them. I show my students my clipboard and that I am putting a star by the name of everyone who shares. When I assure them I won't call on these kids again until everyone else has had a turn sharing in some way, they relax because they know this is fair. Fair is very important to first graders!

Using a High-Frequency Word Chart

The format for modeling and guided practice with our high-frequency word charts is similar to using the ABC chart above. We start the year with kindergarten review words and later put lists with 50 and 100 words in student folders. (See Reproducibles 2, 3, 4.) Each worktable also has a word chart positioned upright with a clear plastic stand (sold at office supply stores). The opposite side of the plastic stand has an alphabet chart that matches our reading series. Children can refer to the charts to spell high-frequency words when writing.

Kobe uses a high-frequency word chart to spell have.

Modeled Writing: What Is a Sentence?

I have been modeling the broad concept of getting our words down in print. Now, and throughout the year, I will focus on the concept of a sentence. The easiest way for me to describe this to first graders is as follows:

- Tell something about a topic; write it down. (Start this idea with a capital and end with a period.)

- Tell something new about the topic; write it down. (Start again with a capital and end with a period.)

- Repeat.

For this early mini-lesson, I use modeled writing on chart paper with three different colored pens (to distinguish each separate sentence), and think aloud as I go through the steps:

1. "I want to tell you three things about my sister and write a sentence for each. First, *My sister is nice*. My first word is *my*, so I'll make the "m" a capital to show the beginning of a new idea." I write the rest and ask, "Did I tell a complete thought about my sister? Did it make sense and sound right? When I am done telling, I put a period to show I am stopping with that idea."

2. "Now, I want to tell something new: *We play ball*. I know this is new because playing is different than my sister being nice. What is my first word that needs a capital in *We play ball*? [Students call out responses.] OK, I'll capitalize the "w" in *we* because that is the first letter in my new sentence." I quickly model writing the sentence (in a different color pen) with "two-finger" spaces, and then dramatically put the period at the end.

3. "Next, I want to tell about swimming at the pool. Is this a new idea from playing ball? [Students respond.] Yes! Remember, every new idea starts with a capital and ends with a period when we are done telling." I choose another color pen and purposefully write *We* on the same line as the previous sentence. "Look, I have room to write the beginning of my sentence about the pool on this line—I don't want to waste paper." I finish writing *We go to the pool and swim* with two-finger spaces and a dramatic period at the end.

Modeled Writing: Each sentence tells a new idea.

My sister is nice. We play ball. We go to the pool and swim.

4. Finally, I remind students: "I am going to be looking for writers today who start each new idea with a capital letter and end it with a period for a stop sign. See if you can tell three or more things about your topic like I did."

Interactive Writing

Interactive writing is a powerful strategy that can start early in first grade through mini-lessons. This is different from modeled writing where I write in front of the class. During a mini-lesson with interactive writing, I share the pen with first graders to create a text together on a chart. This gives me the chance to pack the lessons with the craft of composing and with practice in getting thoughts from our head into words, sounds, and print.

Interactive writing helps first graders as they learn the following writing skills:

- *Deciding what to write*

- *Matching print to speech*
    Hearing sounds in words
    Connecting sounds to letters
    Applying concepts and conventions of print
    Separating words in print with spaces
    Left-to-right directionality
    Return sweep
    Recognizing common rimes/word families

Before starting an interactive writing mini-lesson, I recommend you gather the following materials:

- *chart paper*

Note: You'll want to create a place for teaching points separate from the text. I suggest: fold the paper up from the bottom and use the top half for teaching points and the bottom half for the text we create together; or draw a vertical line to the left and use that area as a teaching space. (See right.) Alternatively, you could have a small whiteboard nearby to make quick teaching points.

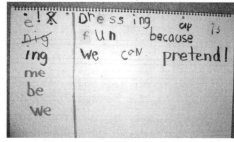

A chart with a teaching area on the left

- *masking tape, clips, pins or easel* (to support chart paper)
- *broad tip marking pens*
- *correction tape* (I prefer 1" Post-It® tape available at office supply stores); Kids call it "boo-boo" tape.
- *pointer* (an unsharpened pencil, a short dowel, or even a fancy wand)
- *ABC chart*
- *classroom names chart*

Names can be links to: beginning sounds, blends, digraphs, rimes, vowel sounds, capitalization of proper nouns, etc.

STEPS IN INTERACTIVE WRITING

1. Establish the Topic

classroom news
short science observations
social studies reports
literature responses
food items needed for a class party or cooking project
a letter to the principal/cook/librarian
other topics of interest

2. Establish the Text Length and Format

Length: Short
Interactive writing is brief because it is time intensive to create a text letter by letter and word by word. If we need to add more, it can be done at another time in the day or be continued as the next day's mini-lesson.

List Format: one word or phrase at a time

Narrative Format: one sentence at a time
Actual wording is a joint endeavor between the students and me; however, I can influence word choice by establishing a sentence opener or generating a lead-up discussion that focuses on specific words or concepts. Once we have narrowed down

our topic, I ask, "How can we write that?" When a sentence is agreed upon, the group counts the words in the sentence and "puts the words on their fingers." The fingers represent the separate, spoken words, and the spaces between fingers are easily compared to the spaces that will be created between each word on the chart paper. Early in first grade, students may not be phonemically aware of the separate words in the stream of speech. Saying the sentence slowly and putting each word on a finger makes this process visual and kinesthetic.

3. Write the Text

The agreed-upon text is written word by word. With my guidance, the first graders write all they possibly can and I fill in as needed. A student might write one letter in the word, part of the word, or the entire word—especially if it is a known high-frequency word. There are many tasks and roles in creating the text:

the writer, who adds to the text or puts in punctuation

the spacer, who puts a hand between words (but bends down or stays to the side so the class can see the writer)

the "teacher," who leads the group in reading the text composed so far

A writer and a "spacer" add to our list of school rules.

4. Maintain a Correct Model

Unlike the writing that first graders do in their journals in which they are encouraged to use phonetic/transitional spelling and write independently, in interactive writing there is an expectation of correctness—an expectation that the finished text will look like text from a published book. Since they are just learning about print and conventional construction of text, it is expected that there will be mistakes that need to be corrected. I use the correction tape to cover errors, then guide each writer to self-correct his/her mistakes. I approach this part of the process in a warm, straightforward "let's fix this" way. Nobody is embarrassed, because even I use "boo-boo" tape on my writing occasionally, and students then see me model the on-going editing and correcting that takes place in real writing.

5. Read the Text

After writing each word, the text is read. Depending on the literacy level of your first graders early in the year, this repetition can help reinforce the relationship between print and speech, develop reading fluency, increase recognition of high-frequency words, and strengthen students' knowledge of letter-sound correspondence.

6. Use the Text for a Purpose

Whenever possible, the finished text can be put to use:

- A letter can be delivered.
- A label can be posted.
- A "to do" list can be used to check off items as they are completed.
- A piece of writing can be posted down low (eye level) to be used by first graders who are "Reading the Room" during reading centers or any other choice time in our day.

Tip

Create an instant "Reading the Room" Center: A skirt hanger (with clips) and a large re-sealable bag can be filled with a variety of pointers and non-prescription (or lens-less) glasses, and your students can begin reading text around the classroom.

Why Write?

There are many reasons to write. Early in first grade, most students tell things that are happening in their life to their family and friends. I want to show the class that we use writing for a variety of purposes. A perfect book for this is *Why Write?* by Daniel Moreton and Samantha Berger, because the simple pictures match simple print. For one of my early reading lessons, I read the entire book and then focus on writing a note as a way to open the lesson.

NOTE-WRITING

1. "A note is written quickly to someone else or to myself. Have you seen me take a yellow sticky note and write down something like this? (I write, *Get more pencils.*) And since we actually do need more pencils, I add, "Can my helper put it on the door for me so I see it at recess? That will remind me to get more pencils next time I go to the office."

2. "Notes can be a reminder. A note needs to tell *who* and *what*. It might also tell *where, when,* or *why.* I think I'll write one to my son Kevin so he knows where to find dinner tonight when he comes home from football practice."

   Who? "I'll put Kevin's name on it so he knows it is for him."

   What? "I'll tell him *pizza.*"

   Where? "I'll tell him to look in the refrigerator in the garage."

3. After this modeling, I inform students, "I am going to be looking for writers today who write someone a quick note." I choose Kiera to share her note at the end of writing.

I model writing a note to my son Kevin.

Dear Miss Richards
I lost my homework
Kiera

Aleks and Lexus use the pattern in I See Colors *to write after their emergent-level reading group.*

Sebastian, Andreas, and Aleks write about the surprise ending of Hairy Bear *by Joy Cowley after working in their developing-level reading group.*

I will revisit *Why Write?* whenever I want a mini-lesson to show another purpose for writing. Soon, I model writing an early version of Response to Literature and give reading groups time the next day to write as a follow up to the book used in guided reading instruction.

I pull out *Why Write?* again in December when the class is going to make gingerbread houses. I write simple directions for them to read and follow—another example of using writing for a specific purpose.

Alyssa checks our directions for the next step to make her gingerbread house.

Adding Details

Let's be honest, first grade writing early in the school year is usually basic and boring. I am always looking for ways to nudge them to add details. The problem is that while a six-year-old can *tell* us an amazing story full of colorful details and images—"The snail was slimy and gross when my sister dropped it into my hand at my grandma's house!—in writing it becomes: *I have a snail.* Remember, the process of getting everything from their minds and mouths down on paper will be our work for the entire school year. So, let's get going with a few ideas to get some details added early in the year. This is when I start the chart titled "First Grade➔Longer Stories" that will be the basis of many mini-lessons. We'll also add to this chart throughout the year.

First Grade➔Longer Stories
1. Details = tell more

DRAW IT, WRITE IT

Looking at our new chart, "First Grade→Longer Stories," I add the first way we can meet that goal: "Details = Tell More." I tell students this means we make our stories longer by adding the interesting details we want the reader to know. I suggest that one way to add details is to use color words and model the following:

1. I draw a picture of myself using a variety of colors and details.

2. Below that, I write what I see. I think out loud about my hair color and style (brown and long) and write about that. I use a color words chart that I have posted on the wall to spell *brown*, and together we quickly read the other color words that are on the chart. I make note of the small gold earrings in the picture and write about them. I think out loud about my blue dress that has stripes up and down and write about that. You get the point!

3. Now, I ask students to draw a picture of themselves exactly as they look in the moment. We do this on sheets of 9" x 12" white art paper, and I remind them to leave room in the bottom half for writing. (For a lesson like this, we step out of our routine of using our journals. We will post our self-portraits and descriptive writing on the bulletin board.)

4. Sharing today will be at tables, with groups doing a "read around." The focus of our comments will be on generating interesting words that make a picture in our minds and match our drawings.

NAME IT (Group students according to your regular procedures.)

Another way to use details to avoid boring writing is to use names. I instruct students, "Turn to the person next to you and tell that person the names of everyone in your family. Go!" Allow a few minutes. "Now, I want you to turn to the person on the other side of you and name all your classmates and other kids you know at school. Ready…go!" Allow more time for naming people at school. "OK. Now, let's see if Mrs. Poppin makes her story interesting with names." My teaching partner writes a (boring) sentence about her cats: "I have 2 cats." Immediately the hands go up to help her add details with names—and colors, too.

The hands go up to help Mrs. Poppin fix her boring sentence!

Details and word choice are critical to good writing, and we will continue with these mini-lessons for many months in first grade. As students are working in Writing Workshop, I will also be conferencing with them. The same questions (*What do they know?* and *What do they need?*) that inform my teaching and provide the focus of my mini-lessons, will also drive my one-to-one conferencing. I ask those same questions about each child and his or her writing.

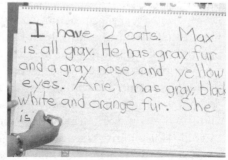

With help from students, details—names and colors—are added.

Conferencing: The First Six Weeks

"If we keep only one thing in mind…it is that we are teaching the writer and not the writing. Our decisions must be guided by 'what might help this writer' rather than 'what might help this writing.' If the piece of writing gets better but the writer has learned nothing that will help him or her on another day on another piece, then the conference was a waste of everyone's time." Lucy Calkins, *The Art of Teaching Writing* (page 158)

Early in the year, I will have two types of conferences. Most will be the traditional Writing Workshop conference to extend and expand the writing. A few first graders will need the more intensive paired-writing to establish the writing task and scaffold concepts about print (letters, sounds, words, spaces). But no matter what issues the conference addresses, it is always about the child. One-to-one conferencing is about the individual learner after all, so we must "follow the child" and meet that learner where he or she is in the writing process—where the child is as a learner and a writer.

Quick Conferences = Differentiation

After the mini-lesson, I roam around the room, checking in with the class. I have done a mini-lesson and will be looking to see who might be trying the next steps that were modeled. But of course, I always look at each student's writing with that lens: *What does she know?* and *What does she need?* Following are samples from two first graders, Lexus and Aleks, on the same day early in first grade and the conference we have based on their writing. This is the range we see every day as we move around the classroom. The beauty of Writing Workshop is that we can truly scaffold our conferences to meet each student's needs—real differentiation every day.

> gos is cre

Lexus writes: "Ghost is scary."

First I meet with Lexus. *What does she know?* I remind Lexus of all the good writing she has done: Lexus tells an exciting story. She spells by the sounds she hears, including long vowels (*gos/ghost* and *cre/scary*). Lexus knows how to spell the important, high-frequency word *is*. She writes from left to right like in books.

What does she need? Lexus needs to expand on this by adding details. We chat briefly about what scary sounds the ghost made. I ask, "What did the ghost do? Did it scare some of her friends? Who?" She plans a new idea: "I told my friends." I have her repeat that to get it solidly in her mind. Then I move on to Aleks.

Aleks writes: "When I go to the school
When I go to the playground
I see ants."

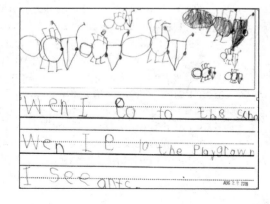

What does he know? I remind Aleks of all the good writing he has done: He has a detailed picture of the ants. He spells many words in standard form (*I, go, to, the, school, see, ants*). The few approximated spellings are matches to sounds (*wen/when*) or use another common spelling pattern for a sound (*playgrown/playground*).

What does he need? I am looking at his illustration and decide to have this be my focus for more descriptive language. I have him describe the ants—what they look like and what they are doing. Aleks is an ELL (Romanian), and I want to hear his oral language and use it as a springboard for more writing. He has lots more to say, and before I leave, I teach a quick skill. We look at the word "wen" (for *when*), and I show him the high-frequency word chart that has it (Reproducible 6). Aleks is ready for the 50 words chart *now* and won't have to wait for the rest of the class who are still using the kindergarten review list of 20 words (Reproducible 2). Conferencing gives me the flexibility to differentiate immediately.

Naturally, my clipboard is at hand as I do conferencing. I am using two forms. The top page is the two-week Writing Workshop Record form (Reproducible 6) with shorthand notes for:

Date

Mini-lesson for that day

Small area for a note

C = Conference

C + = Conference/student is doing well

C – = Conference/Concerns

P = Published

? = Student asked a question

☆ = Student shared

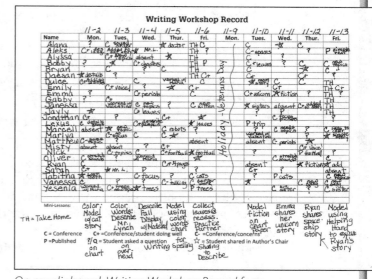

On my clipboard: Writing Workshop Record form

Underneath the Writing Workshop Record form are the Anecdotal Notes sheets for each student. (See pages 16 and 59.) I can jot longer notes here as I conference if needed. Combined, the forms on my clipboard help me keep track of:

• what mini-lesson I did each day

• whom I have conferenced with and how they are doing

• who has shared and who asked questions

• who has published and when

• what their writing looks like over time in a variety of genres

• patterns in their writing that need praise or improvement

Basic Content Conference

Donald Graves stressed this format with all ages of writers, and I have used it ever since with first graders. (I've adapted this format from the one Graves presented at his Dublin conference. See also Reproducible 9.)

LISTEN	I look at a student's face and ask him to tell me about his writing. If I look at the writing first, my mind goes to correctness (handwriting, spaces, spelling, capital, periods) before content. I ask him to read to me a part he wants help with or a section he is proud to share. I *listen* to his writing so I can respond to the content.
TELL BACK	I summarize and retell what my first grader has read. This paraphrase is vital to give the student a big picture of what he has written. Sometimes, students are so focused on *this word* or *this sentence* that they forget what they are writing.
ASK QUESTIONS	There are three basic types of questions that clarify, expand, and extend the writing: "I don't understand…" (CLARIFY) "Tell me more about…" (EXPAND) "What do you plan next…" (EXTEND)

Do I dare teach a new skill before I move on? Sure! One quick skill that a student desperately needs is OK to add, even if he or she hasn't mastered all the basic skills, like spaces, sounds, high-frequency words, capitals, or periods. Conferencing can be like triage at the Emergency Room: I deal with the most critical needs first. My focus is what will most help *this* writer and what she needs now that will take her the furthest. If it turns out a student needs *everything*, he or she is a perfect candidate for the occasional "paired writing conference."

Paired Writing: Conferencing With Emergent Writers and English Language Learners

"Paired writing" was developed by Helen Depree, who helped Marie Clay develop Reading Recovery®. I am especially grateful for this intense intervention for a very emergent writer in first grade. (The Reading Recovery site at The Ohio State University also created interactive writing as a whole-class or small-group version of paired writing.) I have adapted paired writing to be a choice for a classroom teacher during conferencing. It is a little more time-intensive than a traditional conference, but perfect for those writers who are totally confused about using print, like Ashley.

Ashley writes "MAT" but doesn't know what it says when we conference on September 10th. The following Monday, September 14th, she writes "S" and scribbles a drawing in frustration.

The very next day, I intervene with Ashley, and together we create one sentence. Then she adds to her story about our class pet, a beloved white rat named Nibbles. Paired writing can be a quick fix with a student like Ashley, who had transferred in and had not

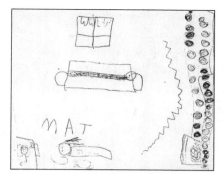

Ashley writes "MAT" but doesn't know what it says.

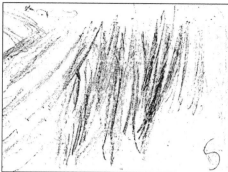

Ashley writes "S" and scribbles with frustration.

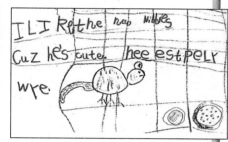

After conferencing, Ashley writes: "I like the new Nibbles 'cause he's cute. He is really white."

been writing in kindergarten. Most emergent writers need an occasional lesson of this intensity over one to three months.

During our paired writing conference, Ashley and I write together: "I like the new Nibbles 'cause he's cute." Ashley continues to work after I leave and writes, "He is really white"—on her own!

INCORPORATING PAIRED WRITING IN YOUR CONFERENCES

I have adapted the following format based on the one developed by Helen Depree. (See also Reproducible 10.)

WHO?	Emergent writers in first grade who need extra support to understand the writing process and how to get words down in print. Most young writers do not need this intensive one-to-one help.
WHEN?	During Writing Workshop while a student is trying to write a rough draft. Parents, volunteers, and upper-grade buddies can be trained to help in class with paired writing using steps 1–5 (below).
MATERIALS?	They are all ready in each student's writing folder: Student's journal, ABC Chart, High-Frequency Word Chart

HOW?	(These five steps provide a one-to-one Tier 1 Response to Intervention lesson.)
	
	1. Have a brief conversation to develop one sentence.
	
	2. Student repeats the sentence to have it firmly in his/her mind.
	
	3. You may need to clap the words and have students count them on their fingers.
	
	4. Work word by word with the student:
	
	  • *Stretch word orally (rubber-band writing) What do you hear first? Do you know what letter makes that sound? Can you make it? What do you hear next?*
	
	  • *Student records everything he/she can, letter by letter.*
	
	  • *Mistakes are covered with "boo-boo" tape.*
	
	  • *Teacher/volunteer fills in the letters that are unfamiliar to the student* (to make an accurately spelled word and/or sentence).
	
	  • *Take a few simple, phonetic words "to boxes," or take a few high-frequency words "to fluency."* (See below.)
	
	  • *Student rereads the entire sentence after each word is added.*
	
	5. Establish what the student will write next and leave the student to work independently. Do this occasionally, only as needed.

PAIRED-WRITING STRATEGY: TAKE "TO BOXES"

This refers to "Elkonin Boxes," which provide a visual representation for each sound. They are named after D.B. Elkonin, a Russian psychologist who pioneered their use in segmenting words into individual sounds for phonological awareness.

How to use "Boxes"

1. From the student's written sentence, choose a word with four or fewer sounds to write (e.g., "cat")

2. Ask the child to repeat the word slowly.

3. Draw "boxes" or squares on a practice area, with one box for each sound.

4. Show the child how to push a finger into each box while making each sound in the word: /c/ /a/ /t/

5. The child fills in the letters he or she knows, and the teacher fills in any others, as needed.

PAIRED-WRITING STRATEGY: TAKE "TO FLUENCY"

Another helpful strategy for teaching high-frequency words is taking a word "to fluency." To take a word to fluency, the student writes a high-frequency word several times in a practice area quickly. For instance, *my* in the examples that follow, I show Rodrigo how to write "my," then it is time for him to practice. I have him "write it here," "write it again over there," then write it again—and each time I cover up the ones he has already written. This is a game-like format but helps ensure the word is known as a whole and can be produced fluently.

PAIRED-WRITING PROGRESS OVER TIME

Let's look at the progress paired writing can make between September and February. In the examples below, Rodrigo, a Spanish-speaking ELL, takes on more of the writing task over time as I do paired writing with him occasionally. If using an unlined journal, the blank page on the left becomes a teaching/practice area. Or you can use a small whiteboard for the teaching/practice area. When using the "boxes" strategy, words with letters in boxes in the practice area are sounded out letter by letter. The boxes give a visual representation of each sound in a word and are an important scaffold. With the "fluency" strategy, the high-frequency word is written several times on the side and practiced for mastery. Creating a bank of written words builds fluency in writing. The practice area can also be used to teach how to form a letter, work on a word pattern/rime, or use the analogy strategy to link new words to known words (*see/bee*).

Rodrigo is one of those teacher-pleasing new first graders whose early writing needs a closer look. He looked like a busy writer but I discovered that he was copying names and color words off charts and other print around the room. That is certainly a good start, but I did paired writing with him to show him how to get *his* words down in print.

In September, Rodrigo wants to write "My pet is a

Rodrigo's early writing was copying.

black cat." I teach him *my* on the practice area and he writes it several times for fluency. He knows the "p" and "t" in *pet,* and I fill in the middle. He can write the "i" in *is,* and I fill in the "s," pointing out that it makes the sound of /z/. Rodrigo can write the word *a*, and I fill in *black* (although Rodrigo was copying color words, he didn't know which was "black"). We take *cat* to boxes so he learns to segment a short word.

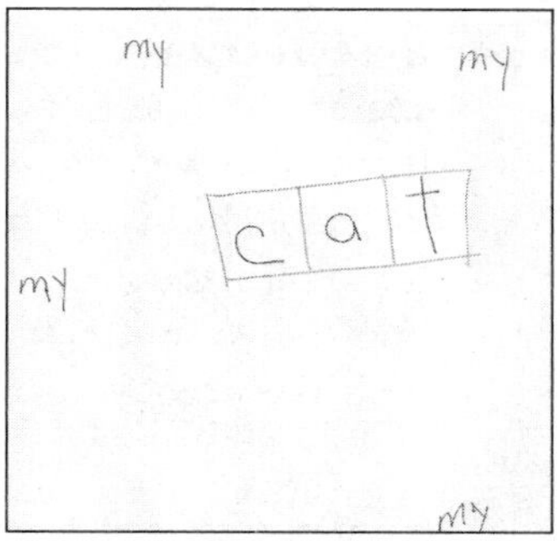

Paired Writing: Practice Area in September

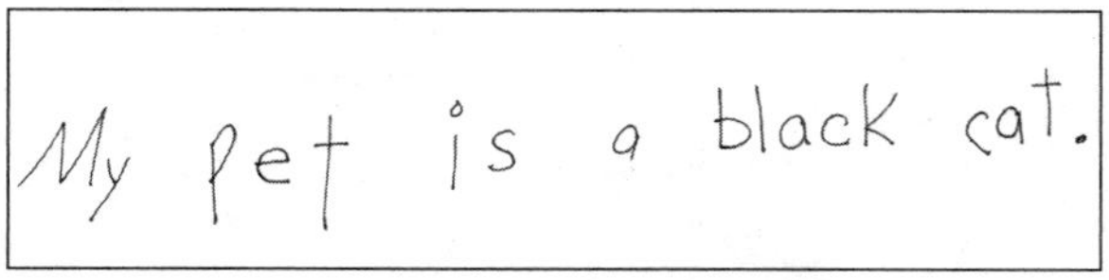

With help, Rodrigo writes about his black cat.

We do paired writing whenever possible, and Rodrigo makes a great deal of progress that I can show his parents at November conferences. In December, we talk about his holiday plans, and he decides to write about Grandma's puppy. He now can quickly write the high-frequency words, *I, to, see,* and *my*, so his independence is increasing daily. We take *want* to fluency to add to his bank of known words. I take the word *see* to the practice area and show Rodrigo how he can write other words with this common pattern. Analogy (using something known to write something new) is a huge part of building confident writers and readers. We use analogy again when writing *Grandma*. Rodrigo knows the word *and* in the middle, so he learns that words he knows might be part of bigger words he is learning. We do a word he knows in boxes: *cup*. I make the link to *pup* for his story. He starts the word *puppy* with the beginning he knows, and I add the second syllable. At this point, I've done enough teaching for one lesson; I don't want to overwhelm him.

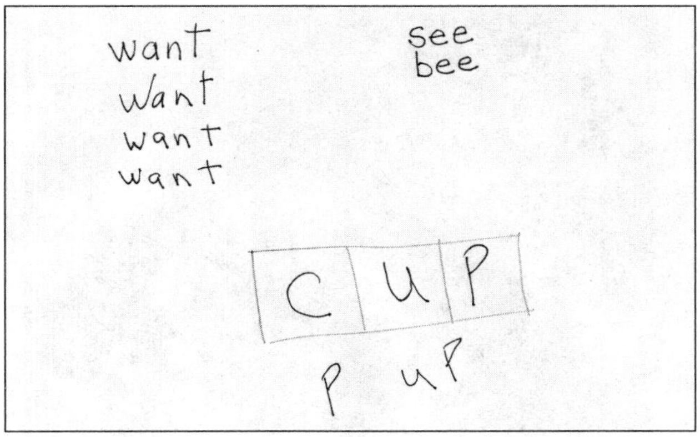

In a December paired-writing conference, Rodrigo takes "cup" to boxes and uses analogy to spell "pup." He uses the "ee" pattern to spell "see" and "bee", and takes "want" to fluency.

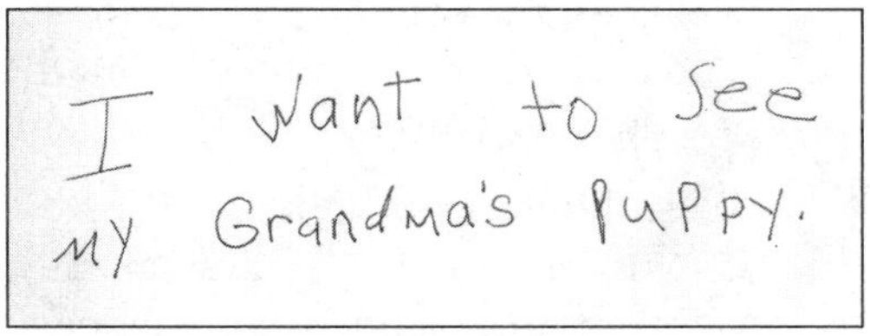

The result of our paired-writing conference: a complete sentence with new words

In February, Rodrigo is excited to write about plans for our class Valentine's Day party. I spend my time extending what he knows about words. He can write classmate Bobby's name, and we use analogy to match the sound/letter at the end of *Bobby, candy* and *party* to establish that *y* at the end of a multi-syllable word makes the long-*e* sound. It turns out that Rodrigo doesn't need such intense paired writing anymore; he is able to pick up this knowledge from our class reading, word work, and spelling lessons. My conferences with Rodrigo can now focus mostly on the craft of writing.

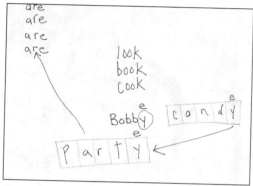

Practice area from another paired-writing conference

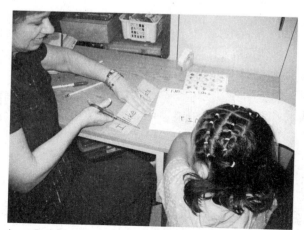

By February, Rodrigo has become an independent writer.

HOW TO MAKE PAIRED WRITING A TIER 2 RESPONSE TO INTERVENTION

This writing-and-reading intervention could be done 3–5 days a week and adds the "cut-up sentence" scaffold to the lesson:

1. Copy the student's sentence on a sentence strip.

2. Cut it up word by word as the student rereads his or her sentence.

3. Mix up the sentence words for student to match to the sentence in his or her writing journal.

4. Mix up the sentence words for student to rebuild on the table without a matching sentence.

5. Send the words home in an envelope with the sentence written on the front for the student to practice at home independently or with a family member.

I put Dulce's sentence on a strip and cut it, word by word, as she reads it.

First Grade Writing Workshop © 2014 Judy Lynch • Scholastic Teaching Resources

Dulce rebuilds the sentence at the top of her journal page with matching as a scaffold.

A proud Dulce shows that she can mix up the words and rebuild her sentence without matching. The words go home in an envelope for more practice.

Troubleshooting Tips

Insecure students, just out of kindergarten, have to be taught how to solve some of their own problems, or even rely on classmates nearby. Otherwise these students will follow you around the room, ask you to spell every word for them, write on the same topic over and over, draw instead of write—and probably drive you crazy!

PROBLEM: They follow me around the room.

Early in first grade, I feel like the Pied Piper when I see students following me around the room. Some need assurance that each thing they have written is correct and makes Mrs. Lynch happy. Others can't spell a word and want it done now. First graders often look to the teacher to validate every action. It can be quite a process to move them from feeling and acting helpless to being independent, confident problem solvers.

SOLUTION: Early in first grade I do a mini-lesson about what to do when students need help.

We make a chart to use as a reference and the ideas come from them:

WHEN I NEED HELP IN WRITING	
Read my story again. ➪	Add to my story.
Look at my picture. ➪ Ask my neighbor quietly. Look at my ABC and Word Charts. Write something new. Stay in my seat. Help myself.	Add to my story.

PROBLEM: They all want me at once.

Soon first graders are staying in their seats and building writing stamina. As I move about the room conferencing, often those seated nearby want my attention all of a sudden, too.

SOLUTION: Include those nearby in the conference.

If appropriate and they can benefit from listening in, I invite a few students to join our conference. This officially sanctioned eavesdropping can help more than just the student with whom I am having the chat. This work becomes a model lesson that many others usually need, too.

PROBLEM: They want me to spell for them.

SOLUTION: "3 Ways to Spell a Word"—Word Wall/Word Charts;
            Arm Spelling; Rubber-Band Writing

Teaching students strategies to try to spell words themselves is critical in helping them become independent writers. (It is also essential for *your* sanity!) In order for it to happen, though, the steps towards independence must be consistent.

Bring Parents on Board

I am usually the first adult who won't spell for kids because parents do it for them at home. It is crucial to explain to parents at Back to School Night that in first grade *students need to attempt to spell a word on their own first* because it uses their phonics knowledge and will help with writing and reading. As part of this quick parent training, I show copies of one child's work over several months when students take on responsibility for spelling. Parents come on board when they can see that first graders use exciting word choice with topics like "Tyrannosaurus rex" (*tirnusorus rx*) rather than "dogs" and "butterflies" (*bdrfliz*) rather than "bugs." I make a version of my "3 Ways to Spell a Word" poster (see page 53) to give to parents. I explain how to use it at home. They can see how we work on correct spelling of the most common words used in writing with our word wall. I show the two ways their first grader can attempt to sound-spell: using "arm spelling" for short words and "rubber-band writing" for longer words. With these strategies and the ABC chart and high-frequency word charts I pass out, parents can help their child learn to spell words at home. Parents always appreciate receiving copies of high-frequency word lists. I also explain to parents that the final editing for any published writing will produce totally correct spelling—and parents breathe a sigh of relief because they are assured I am teaching spelling!

Bring First Graders on Board

I do a very early mini-lesson about why I don't spell for them. I tell students to pretend they all need help spelling a word and to raise their hand. I then tear around the room dramatically spelling for each child while *the entire class waits to be helped,* and I keep looking at my watch to time the process. When we debrief, they get the idea that this is a total waste of their time for writing. I also add, "Did Alyssia, Daesen, Jonathon, Sarah, Misty, Bobby, Janessa, Oliver, etc., learn how to spell their words when I did it for them? No way! I was just getting exercise as I hurried to do the work for them."

Post "3 Ways to Spell a Word" on a Bulletin Board—or Anywhere in the Room

I make and display a large poster of "3 Ways to Spell a Word" and *refer to it for months.* The first week of school, we learn five new word wall words, and I refer to the poster. When I do my mini-lesson on using the ABC Chart, we look at the poster. When I do a mini-lesson on arm spelling short words, we look at the poster. When I do a mini-lesson on the word chart with 20 kindergarten review words, we look at the poster. "3 Ways to Spell a Word" is an anchor chart on spelling for the rest of the year.

---

3 WAYS TO SPELL A WORD

1. Look at the Word Wall.

2. Sound out a short word on my arm.

3. Sound out a long word like a rubber band.

PROBLEM: They write about the same thing day after day.

SOLUTION: Declare them an "expert" on that topic.

Donald Graves was asked at that conference at St. Patrick's College in Dublin years ago: "We know they should get topic choice, but what if they write about the same topic ad nauseam?" Graves, practical and brilliant, simply said to *declare them an expert on the topic and move them on*. I remembered this when I was worried about Marcel early in first grade because he wrote daily about his favorite thing to draw: Sponge Bob Square Pants. To tell the truth, his pictures were improving but not his writing.

While conferencing, I announced that Marcel is our expert on Sponge Bob Square Pants. Part of the reason for this public announcement was that at recess he could advise anyone who wanted to write on that topic. "Since he has already completely and totally covered everything about Sponge Bob, he is going to write about new ideas." The next day, he had a gecko on his shirt, so that became his next topic. For the mini-lesson, Marcel was at the front of the room, and the class was giving him ideas about what to write about geckos. I took notes on a small whiteboard: *skin like a lizard, climbs, tongue shoots out*, etc. When we were done, I gave Marcel the whiteboard to remind him about geckos when he was writing. I made notes on my clipboard and checked in often to get him started. It turned out, he connected best with concrete objects, and in the spring he was fascinated with ladybugs. This piece of writing shows the amazing growth Marcel made over many months.

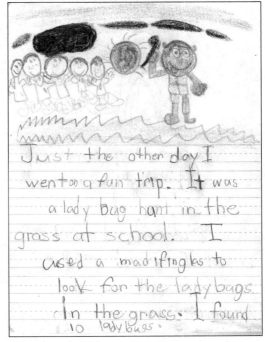

Marcel writes on an exciting new topic in spring: ladybugs!

PROBLEM: All they want to do is draw.

We all know that a drawing can be critical as a springboard for writing. It gives a visual scaffold for students to use. What I find, however, is there might be a few first graders who will spend all their time drawing. They know that writing also tells the story but become immersed in the illustration. It's time for a compromise.

SOLUTION: Divide the paper in half with room for both.

In a mini-lesson, I model drawing a line to separate the top of a page (for the picture) from the bottom (for the text). I set a timer for 5 minutes and explain that I will get right to work and try to draw a complete picture in that time. When the timer goes off, I start to write my story about the big tree in front of my house.

When they write and I start conferencing, I check who starts to write after the timer goes off. I do this for just a few days. I don't want there to be a "5-minute rule" that everyone has to follow. The idea of a space and time for drawing is usually enough for those who need it, and they'll get personal, gentle reminders from me if they need it.

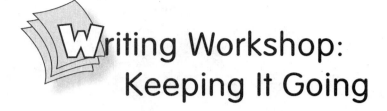

CHAPTER 3

Writing Workshop: Keeping It Going

Getting Help

One of the many nice things about Writing Workshop is that it is structured in a way that enables you to manage it on your own. But with a class full of six-year-olds, you've surely had moments when you think, "Help! There's only one of me!" Busy as you are, how can you make sure you are making the most of Writing Workshop all year long? Getting some occasional assistance makes a great deal of sense! I love to have parent volunteers and even buddies from our upper-grade classes give me a hand. I get their helping hands, and my eager first grade writers get their listening ears. And the larger the audience is for emergent writers, the better! So get parents and buddies trained and organized.

Organizing Parents

I send home a "Parent Volunteer Form" the first week of first grade to alert parents and families to the many ways they can help our class.

The Parent Volunteer form is a generic call for help for the year, but it includes Writing Workshop on a list of possible ways volunteers can assist our class. The second or third week of school, I send home a letter specifically about Writing Workshop that gives more details about how families can help with writing in school or at home. Adapt these to create your own letters to send home with students.

Organizing Buddies

Some years I don't get any parent volunteers or my recruits fade away after a while. No problem! Another great resource is the capable 4th–6th graders at my school. I alert the 4th–6th grade teachers that I am recruiting assistants for Writing Workshop. I send an e-mail to my colleagues or put a letter in their office mailboxes, requesting their help and asking if they have some responsible students they could recommend.

Parent Volunteer Form

First Grade truly appreciates the involvement and support of parents and families. Below are some of the ways our class could use help both inside and outside the classroom. Please fill out the this form and have your child return it to me. The information you provide will help me plan our learning activities throughout the year. Thank you for getting involved in your child's education!

Your name(s) _____

Student's Name _____

Phone number(s) _____ Best times to call _____

Email _____

I would like to help with my child's class by:

❑ Helping students in the classroom during Writing Workshop (training provided!)
❑ Typing simple stories at home for publication (training provided!)
❑ Helping students in the classroom during reading (training provided!)
❑ Recording a story book at home as part of our Mystery Reader Program
❑ Sharing a favorite book, hobby, or career with the class (Note details below.)
❑ Preparing crafts and activities, etc., inside the classroom
❑ Preparing crafts or activities at home
❑ Donating magnetic letters, printer ink or other items for special projects
❑ Helping with special events inside the classroom
❑ Chaperoning a field trip
❑ Donating food items for special events or projects
❑ Other (Note details below.)

I would like to help in one or more of the above ways:
❑ more than once a week   ❑ once a week   ❑ once a month   ❑ occasionally

If there are certain days and/or times that you are available please list below, or add other comments or questions:

_____
_____
_____
_____
_____

Be a Writing Workshop Volunteer!

Dear Parents/Families,

I would love to have your help with Writing Workshop in my class this year. Writing Workshop is an important part of your child's first grade curriculum. There are many ways to volunteer at school or from home. Please let me know if you might be able to participate in some of the ways listed below. If you can, simply fill out the form and have your child return it to me. Your help will be greatly appreciated!

Supplies: Can you donate special colored pencils, fancy crayons, or fine point colored markers? We will use them for illustrating our first grade published books.

❑ YES, I will send some illustration supplies.

Volunteer in Class: Can you volunteer one day a week to help during our

writing time from _____ to _____ ?

I will train all the volunteers so you will feel comfortable working with first grade writers.

❑ YES, I can work on: M T W TH F

❑ NO, but I may be available once in awhile to help in class.

Help From Home: We also need parents who can copy or type simple, short stories at home. I will provide the format to follow and each story should take no more than 20 minutes. If several parents offer to do this, it would be just an occasional job. A big perk is that first graders love to have a parent be our "Publisher."

❑ YES, please sign me up to type short books at home.

Thank you so much!

Your Name: _____   Student's Name: _____

Phone: _____   Email: _____

Questions or Comments: _____

Training Helpers

Giving family members or student buddies a brief training session gives them the guidelines and confidence to be productive volunteers in our classroom.

Materials:

I train upper-grade students during class so I can model the process.

I make copies of some essential forms, lists, and procedures that my volunteers may need, and I keep them in a handy folder. Here are some that I include:

- Review Words to Start the Year (Reproducible 2)
- 50 High-Frequency Words (Reproducible 3)
- 100 High-Frequency Words (Reproducible 4)
- A copy of "What First Grade Writers Need to Know to Get Started" (page 19)
- Content Conference Guide (Reproducible 9)
- Paired-Writing Guide (Reproducible 10)
- A copy of "3 Ways to Spell a Word" (page 53)
- A copy of "What First Grade Writers Need to Know to Keep Going" (page 64)

When and How?

Usually I try to train parents on a school day right after school for about 45 minutes. Evening meetings are also an option. Buddies are usually trained during class because they ride the bus home after school or walk younger children home. There are some basic guidelines I cover with both.

1. Overview of Writing in First Grade

Using the Content Conference Guide and the "What First Grade Writers Need to Know to Keep Going" chart, I can give parents and buddies an idea of what it is like to work with budding writers who are limited in spelling and just learning the craft of putting ideas down on paper. These two guides give helpers an idea of where we are and where we are going.

2. Spelling for First Grade Writers

"3 Ways to Spell a Word" clearly shows the three ways to spell a word. As further resources, I use the high-frequency word lists. Helpers can be taught how to refer to these lists and our ABC chart when a first grader is trying to spell a word. Rather than just mindlessly spelling every word for them, we can model strategies that students can learn to use independently.

Everyone who will be working in Writing Workshop has to be on the same page—so to speak. Right away, they need to understand how important it is not to just go

First Grade Writing Workshop © 2014 Judy Lynch • Scholastic Teaching Resources

ahead and spell for first graders—unless it is a final edit for publishing. Often "helpful" parents and buddies don't understand this at first, so I explain that if we spell words for them all the time, all they learn is to write the letters that someone else tells them. We are teaching for independence, which means using the resources available to them in their folder (ABC and high-frequency word charts) or in the room (word wall, color and number word charts, etc.) to learn how to spell words.

3. Conferences for the Content of Student Writing

I like to give helpers a sticky note with the names of those students they should work with that day. The note will have a "C" after student names who urgently need help with the *content/craft* of writing.

Who? First Graders who need to expand on their ideas and add details.

When? During writing when a student has written a short piece

How? (In training, model this process with a first grader):

Spend 3–5 minutes with each student listening to his/her story and asking questions to nudge them further in adding to their topic. Use the Content Conference Guide or the training. Have volunteers *listen, tell back,* and *ask questions.* Reflection on what the student knows or needs is left to you, the teacher.

LISTEN	Look at the writer's face. Ask the student to tell you about his or her writing. As appropriate, suggest: "Read me the part you want help on" or "Read me the part you are proud of."
TELL BACK	Summarize what the student has read so it is firm in his or her mind.
ASK QUESTIONS/ COMMENT	"I don't understand…" (CLARIFY) "Tell me more about…" (EXPAND) *Who? What? When? Where? Why? How?* (DETAILS) "What do you plan next…" (EXTEND)

4. Paired Writing for the Most Emergent Writers

As I said before, I give volunteers a sticky note with the names of those students they should work with that day. The note will also have a "PW" after student names when paired writing is the most appropriate help. I inform my volunteers that they will spend more time with these students, perhaps 10 minutes, and use the Paired-Writing Guide as a resource.

Who? Emergent writers who need extra support to understand the writing process and how to get ideas/sentences/words/letters down in print. Most young writers do *not* need this intensive one-to-one help.

Where? A reading table over to the side of the room is the best place for this longer conference.

When? During writing while a student is trying to write a sentence.

How? (In training, model this process with a first grader):

1. Have a brief chat to develop one sentence. Possible topics: favorite foods, games, friends, family, pets, trips

2. Student repeats the sentence so it is firmly in mind.

3. You may need to clap the words and have the student count them on his/her fingers.

4. Work with student, word by word, on the following:
   –Stretch a word orally, letter by letter; refer to ABC chart. Ask "What do you hear first? What do you hear next?"
   –Student records everything he/she can.
   –Fill in the letters that are unfamiliar to the student to form an accurately spelled word/sentence.
   –Student rereads the entire sentence after each word is added, pointing under each word.

5. If time allows, put the words on a sentence strip for the student.
Materials to have on hand: *sentence strips, scissors, envelopes*
As the student reads a sentence to you, cut it apart into words. Mix up the words and have the student rebuild the sentence (using the original as a guide). Write the sentence on an envelope (with words inside) for student to take home to practice.

Advanced Training Topics

When I need help with publishing, I will train volunteers to assist with the process described in Chapter 4. Sometimes they will help with the final edit or type the story into the computer.

Parents and upper-grade students can be valuable resources in Writing Workshop. Be creative in using them to help you model the writing process for beginning writers. Don't be shy about asking your volunteers to share their own writing with the class (*grocery lists, work products, letters*, etc.). That way, students can see writing as a part of all of our lives.

As a mini-lesson on writing nonfiction, older buddies can share their own writing with the class. When this happens, my first graders eagerly ask questions.

A buddy helps with editing.

Assessment: How Are They Doing?

Assessment, both informal and formal, drives our instruction in Writing Workshop in first grade. The key to productive assessment is multiple sources of information:

- Anecdotal Notes
- Skills Chart
- District Writing Continuum
- Common Core State Standards
- Teacher Judgment

Anecdotal Notes for Informal Assessment

The Writing Workshop Records and the Anecdotal Notes I take on a regular basis are described in Chapter 1. I look at each child's writing in depth to look for progress, needs, and trends. This information becomes a key element for writing comments for report cards and for conferencing with parents.

Name: Jonathon					
DATE	CONTEXT	ANECDOTAL NOTES	WHAT DOES HE/SHE KNOW?	WHAT DOES HE/SHE NEED?	
8-12 to 8-15	1st Week	He worked 3 days on a detailed account of their trip to Canada.	• sequence • many high freq. words • accurate phonetic spelling	Praise his sense of storytelling and detail	Publish later
Early Sept.	He is trying to add color words	His writing is short and stilted — he is following the mini-lesson on colors	He thinks he needs detailed pictures now	He needs to know it is OK to break loose with a story & skip the picture if he wants	
Oct.	Daily Writing	Spurts of writing but more detail in pictures. Lacks focus	• brainstormed ghost story using Helping Hand	• sustained effort • transfer brain-storming into sentence form	
12-3	He noticed other kids were trying Christmas stories	Very patterned & stilted "I like Christmas." "It is fun"	He has noticed others writing like this and is copying their style	• Conference with him using detailed story from week #1 to compare • Praise him for his own "style"	
1-7	Lost Tooth Story	J. has a sense of drama "I lost my tooth!!!"	• Sequences the main events • Uses a variety of sentences — not patterned or stilted	• d/b reversals need to be taken care of with letter sorting • Praise the style	
3-02	Started a longer fiction piece	Looks like a copy ("Half Blud Theifs") but the story seems original in the biggest sense.	• Telling story in first person • Very dramatic desription of "parents"	• He has written the first chapter. • Write him a note to meet and talk about what comes next. Not ready to publish yet	

Anecdotal Notes for Jonathon, August – March

Using the Skills Chart for Informal Assessment

The "Skills ____ Can Do as a Writer" chart (Reproducible 11) can be used throughout the year when looking at student work. I make copies on cardstock, fill in the name, and keep them in each student's writing folder so I can use them while conferencing with the student. When I first started writing with first graders, these charts helped me check that standards were being met. I make sure students know that their writing over time has to show a benchmark being met, which is then celebrated, recorded, and dated. You can also use your own district and/or Common Core standards list in each folder and date them.

District Writing Continuum

My school district has a powerful First Grade Writing Continuum that evaluates each student's writing developmentally. It is the middle piece of a continuum that begins in kindergarten and continues through second grade. We use it to score district-wide responses to writing prompts three times a year and assess the responses within the range from "Far Below Basic" to "Advanced." But I also use it to do report cards, evaluating each first grader's writing over time rather than on a one-shot writing prompt. You may want to use your school district's continuum guideline for assessing your students. For this longitudinal view of the current trimester, I use the student's Writing Workshop journal, my anecdotal notes, and the "Skills _____ Can Do as a Writer" chart for multiple measures of growth. During this report card process, I also put small sticky notes on key writing exemplars in each student's journal to share with parents at conference time. Using a continuum shows me where they are now and what they need next. It also informs parents beyond a grade or label.

Common Core State Standards

Besides our state standards, I also look at the Common Core State Standards, discussed in detail in the Introduction. Periodically it is valuable to reflect on both whole-class and individual progress towards these standards, which should be met by the end of first grade. I can plan mini-lessons and focused conferences using this added information.

Teacher Judgment

Of course, informed teacher judgment is at the heart of assessment and teaching. I am informed by multiple sources so that I am confident when preparing mini-lessons, conferencing, writing report card comments, and talking to parents. In my opinion, high-stakes testing has often put the teacher at the sidelines in assessment and placed higher value on one-shot glimpses of student achievement that reduce a six-year-old to a number or a label. I believe that multiple measures, including high-stakes testing, give the most accurate information to inform writing instruction and follow each child. Let's put our assessments to work in planning further mini-lessons (and procedures) and next steps for our class.

Procedures: Beyond the First Six Weeks— Giving First Graders an Audience

Early procedures are in place, but before we get into further mini-lessons, it is important to go over some additional procedures that will be helpful in the coming weeks and throughout the year. I always do a procedural mini-lesson whenever something new is added that needs to be modeled and practiced in detail. Now it is time to give first graders an audience. Here I will focus on two procedures for sharing student writing, as this will be a significant aspect of Writing Workshop from now on.

Author's Chair

The first weeks of school, we do Quick Sharing in front of the class instead of Author's Chair.

I do so many foundational procedures at the start of the year that I wait on this one. However, when it is time to share in more depth and in a more intimate setting on the rug, I break down the process into parts to model and practice. My ideal for Author's Chair is to have the first graders sit in a circle on the rug. The "Author's Chair" itself is usually my teacher chair, although I know many of you may make an adorable chair decorated just for this purpose. This year, I had to throw out my notion of a circle because we now have 28 students and the room is packed with student seating. In order to have room for a circle, the class and I would have to move a lot of furniture each afternoon. Reality hits! So, the kids sit on their bottoms ("criss-cross applesauce") in rows in front of the student who is in the Author's Chair.

The area is packed with first graders eager to hear 6th-grade buddy Alena share her writing about Egypt.

PROCEDURES TO MODEL AND PRACTICE FOR AUTHOR'S CHAIR

Audience:
- How to walk to the sharing area
- Where to sit
- How to sit
- How to listen
  hands folded in lap
  eyes on the author
  ears listening
  thinking about questions and compliments
- How to ask questions

Authors:
- Practice reading beforehand to build fluency and confidence. (Children can practice with an adult, a buddy, or a classmate.)
- Hold your journal so it doesn't cover your face and block your voice.
- Read in an Author's Voice (a clear, loud voice).
- Point to the words to keep your place.
- Hold the book/journal for all to see the pictures.

Plan for loads of practice on how to ask questions, because first graders love to tell more than ask!

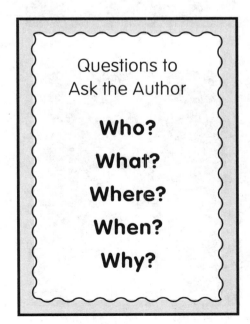

Questions to Ask the Author

Who?

What?

Where?

When?

Why?

An author practices before sharing.

I model how not to read from my journal; No one can see or hear me!

Read in a clear, loud voice.

The balance for all these procedural mini-lessons is to keep them short and revisit as often as necessary over the next several weeks of school. Early on, I sit on a small chair close by and help the author—*but only when absolutely necessary*. Eventually, I try to be a member of the audience and often sit down on the rug with the class to reinforce my role.

Authors learn to show their illustrations to their audience.

Point to the words to keep your place.

Partner Sharing as an Alternative to Author's Chair

Partner sharing works very well because it provides increased feedback for emergent writers. To train for the procedures unique to this format consider doing the following:

Partner Sharing can be an alternative to Author's Chair.

1. Establish partners ahead of time.

2. Have a method for determining who reads first.

3. Model and practice how to offer (anticipated) feedback with:

   I liked _____ (compliment)

   I wonder (*who, what, where, when, why*) _____ (question)

4. Model and practice what to do when each partner has had a turn reading and responding. (Message: Keep going; read an earlier piece.)

5. Have a stop signal.

Mini-Lessons: Beyond the First Six Weeks

Following the Class: What do they know? What do they need?

Throughout the year in first grade, I look for patterns in students' writing that need to be addressed with mini-lessons and followed up with conferences. I am guided by assessments, standards, and "What First Grade Writers Need to Know to Keep Going." This chart (see page 64) reminds me there should always be a balance between the craft and conventions of writing; between what is said and saying it in an understandable way.

An easy trap to fall into is to look at first grade writing, see all the "mistakes," and then drown students in spelling and punctuation mini-lessons. Don't let this happen! Remember to consider first *what they know* and *what they need*. The lens for looking at the class as a whole is still driven by these two questions. For example, you may notice that students are beginning to write sentences or complete thoughts, but you can't read them easily—and neither can they—because they run together. Be sure to applaud their use of complete thoughts and simply add a quick conventions mini-lesson on capitals and end punctuation. If you notice some overall crafting issues, rather than point out problems, you can teach a mini-lesson that addresses it. For example, when I noticed that students needed to use more descriptive language, I chose an account of the cow visiting our school as a model for a lesson on descriptive language. I wrote a boring, nondescript piece first so we could do a comparison. "I saw a cow. The cow is nice. I like the cow." Then, I put up some student writing that included color and size words, and we noted the difference. This is just one of many mini-lessons using descriptive word choice that I will detail later in the chapter.

I also want to show examples of writing that exhibit emotion, personality, and attitude—in other words, the trait of Voice. So whenever I can, I look for writing, such as

What First Grade Writers Need to Know to Keep Going

- Writing needs to make sense.

- The conventions of print help the reader understand the message:
  - spaces
  - legible handwriting
  - capitals
  - punctuation
  - spelling

- Spelling has regular and irregular patterns

- We can use common spelling patterns to spell words

- We can use words we know to spell words that are new (cat helps us spell bat, rat and splat)

- Helpful writing tools include:
  - alphabet cards and alphabet strips
  - wall charts and word walls
  - high frequency word cards
  - simple dictionaries

- To write a complete thought, we start it with a capital and end it with a period.

- Descriptive words make writing more enjoyable to read
  - colors
  - shapes
  - sizes

- We can expand on a topic to write four to six sentences to create a simple paragraph

Marina's (below), that has "oomph." She has that important sense of audience, which is evident when she asks the reader, "Why do you think it is?"

I know that first graders also need concrete objects and clear pictures to write about. I took a picture of orcas off the coast of Washington on a vacation one year. I did a mini-lesson about writing facts by writing about the whales I saw. As an incentive to try this type of writing (informational), I laid my picture on the rug for anyone who wanted to write about it that day. A small group lay on their tummies and wrote about whales for two days. One student not only wrote but used proper punctuation to end three types of sentences! Her writing was on the projector the next day and exemplified the balance between craft and conventions.

Telling
Asking   ?
Excited   !

I got a shot on the thum. why do you thik it is? I know to dec are blud. They mite give you a lolypop. They cary arond candy and tLushops. Shots do sti.

Marina's visit to the doctor

Our Orcauis
Mrs. Lynch autaub a Orcau
for my whole class. Do you know why she did? Because she din't want it to die! Orcaui's are blad and white. Pepole call Orcaui's Killer Wales. Mrs. Lynch took pictures.

Writing about orcas on the day we talked about my photo of orcas.

Encouraging New Topics

As every teacher knows, sometimes students will write about the same topics over and over (until we declare them "experts" and nudge them to move onto something else). And some children may have written about a few topics of interest, but have a hard time coming up with new ideas. This is why it is so important to display and maintain your topic chart. The topic chart from the first week of school is used for several months, and we add to it periodically. We also develop and use other strategies to encourage independence with topic choice.

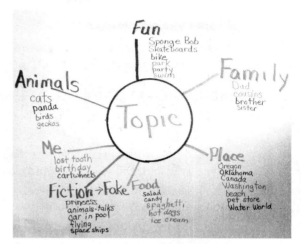

Over time, more topics get added to the chart we started at the beginning of the year.

ADDING TO THE CHART

New topics evolve naturally, and adding them to the chart makes them available to the whole class. For example, someone loses a tooth, and we create a "Me" category that will eventually also include things like birthday stories, sports accomplishments or injuries, etc. When student stories about themselves wane, I introduce fiction ("fake stories") to jazz things up. Soon princess and talking animal stories are popular. Student choice is central to Writing Workshop, but we have to give them an array of experiences and topics from which to choose.

I will still write individual topics in the front of folders when needed. This is especially useful for emergent writers. Janessa, an ELL, needs personal help with new topics. Rather than getting them off the group chart, I write her ideas down for her as we chat, and then we reread them together. Janessa commits to writing about kittens with a check mark.

INDEPENDENT TOPIC CHARTS

Just as some students will need extra support with topics, others are ready for their own personal chart.

I use these charts mid-year with the whole class, but sooner for those who are ready to be more independent. As a mini-lesson, I model using the "My Topics" (Reproducible 12) chart and where students should place it in their folders. The students offer ideas, and as I write them all down, they fill in their charts at the same time. Then they can refer to this list when they need a topic to try.

Mid-year, we brainstorm more topics.

NARROWING TOPICS

It is typical of emergent writers that they choose very broad topics: *My Family, My Vacation, Dogs, Dinosaurs*, etc. To challenge the students who are ready (usually in the spring), I like to do mini-lessons to encourage narrowing a topic. For instance, when we were doing a Science unit on animals, we were preparing to do brief reports. As we brainstormed topics, I worked with students to narrow the focus:

1. Anthony said he wanted to study big cats.

2. I dramatically spread my arms wide and asked, "Do you want to write about ALL the big cats in the world—lions, tigers, cheetahs, jaguars, mountain lions, cougars?" (My arms and words emphasized on how huge the topic would become.)

3. I closed my arms so they are straight in front of me and said, "Maybe you could choose one big cat to study?" (The emphasis now is on how small the topic would become.)

4. Anthony decided to study only cheetahs.

5. Finally, the clincher: I spread my arms again wide and said, "Now can you tell everything there is about cheetahs?" Anthony nodded in agreement. His final product showed his focus for a simple published report.

Bryan writes about the grasshopper he caught.

My Grandpa
My Grandpa Deaded.
July 14. he Was 59 yer old. He Had his leg cat off. he only had hafe of his Heart lefte
a capall day later he Ternd 60.
he alway Bot me Candy.

A grandfather's passing

Writing About What Matters

Mini-lessons throughout first grade will weave in an important message: Writers write about what matters to them, what they care about. I will look for writing samples that make this obvious. We will hear the author's voice when the topic is dear to them. Sometimes it is as simple as a grasshopper found at recess or as profound as a tribute to a dear grandpa's passing.

Sometimes I can nudge students by modeling my own impassioned writing with my strong opinions: "Cars should slow down in front of our school!" "My dog Rebel is the cutest dog in town." "I would rather read than play video games." When children feel strongly about something, it motivates them to write—and their writing is generally of better quality. Since we are also learning about the difference between facts and opinions, expressing opinions is a natural fit for Writing Workshop.

It wud be nice if theaer wus no wars.
It wud be nice if nobude killed whales.
Itu wud be nice if nobude spilld oil becus the Dophins era diing.

Opinion piece: "It would be nice if…"

Word Choice: Adding Description and Details

Vivid words make a picture in the reader's mind. Mini-lessons on word choice are ongoing during the entire school year. Where *description* is a broad term that applies to the entire narrative (providing precise and interesting information about a thing being described), *details* are those few, most effective bits to include from that vast sea of possible description (Haven, 2001). Let's look at some mini-lessons on how students can put details and description in their stories.

RANK IT

Modeling great language with read-alouds is a natural with first graders. Thinking out loud about the author's choice of words brings this idea to the forefront. On the second reading of an engaging story, you can have the student's play "Rank It" with a simple scale: High (+) Medium (√) Low (–). Have them explain their ranking and give examples of the "juicy" words. You can get an all-student response with simple hand signals:

High + Have them make a cross with both index fingers.

Medium √ Have them make a "checking off" motion with one index finger.

Low – Have them hold one index finger horizontally.

SHAPES AND SIZES

I use objects in the classroom to demonstrate elaborating with details. For this mini-lesson, I sat in three chairs of different size, color, and materials. We generated better descriptive words to describe each chair, in detail, one at a time:

I sat on the chair.

I write this on chart paper and have the students give me a thumbs up or down to indicate whether it is an interesting sentence. Ironically, they all give me thumbs up! I tell them, "NO! It is BORING!!" Then I suggest, "Close your eyes. Can you see what this chair might look like or feel like? What more could I have said about the chair?" One student offers:

I sat on the big, blue chair.

Then we can use this sentence to build vocabulary by coming up with other words for "big": *huge, enormous, gigantic.* I plunk myself down in the next chair, and write:

I sat on the little green chair.

We continue to build vocabulary by brainstorming words for "little": *small, tiny, puny.* The third time is usually a charm. When I get to the third chair, the students are already better at including details and description:

I sat on the teacher's chair with the soft, scrunchy cushion.

Follow-up: During conferencing, I follow-up on this mini-lesson by encouraging the use of descriptive words with colors and sizes. When I notice students who have attempted better word choice, I invite them to do an Author's Chair for the class.

FIVE SENSES

Using sensory details will add impact to first grade writing that is in a rut. This way, their audience will not only "see" what happens but may also smell, hear, feel, and taste it, too. Mini-lessons that include food will really get your first graders' attention. As we use the Description: 5 Senses graphic organizer (Reproducible 13), we take time to gather in a circle and brainstorm together what we smell, see, hear, taste, and feel (in that order). This generally requires doing it in steps to make it manageable for first graders:

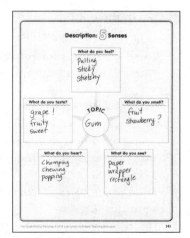

A sample 5-Senses organizer that we used for "gum"

Teacher Models With a Projector or Chart Paper

1. Put the topic item in the center of the chart (for example: gum, popcorn, orange slices).

2. Start with, "What do you smell?" and go clockwise from student to student.

3. Model taking down notes for each sense, and then write a group story together.

On another topic on the next day. . .

Students Practice Taking Notes While Teacher Models

4. Model all senses for a new item for the class, this time with students taking notes.

5. Ask for volunteers to read their notes and model how to turn each "note" into a sentence.

On another topic on another day. . .

Everyone Takes Notes and Writes

6. Brainstorm a new topic together. Take turns providing sensory descriptions of all five senses. Everyone takes notes, then students write individually, with a partner, or with a small group that needs extra support.

STICKER STORIES

We know first graders write better with a picture for support. A twist on this is to provide a simple sticker to describe. For the mini-lesson, I model how to do this activity:

1. Choose one sticker.

2. Place it on the top half of your journal page.

3. Using crayons, draw details around the sticker to make a complete illustration.

4. On the bottom half of the journal page, write about your drawing, using as many details as possible.

I will keep the stickers available as a choice throughout the year and replenish periodically.

Sticker story: "Winnie the Pooh"

Sticker story: "Dinosaur"

SHOW AND TELL

For many years, I dreaded "Show and Tell" but recognized how developmentally important oral language is in first grade. Sweet relief came when I linked "Show and Tell" to Writing Workshop. If a student brought something to share (that precious rock, soccer trophy, birthday present, etc.), the class would ask questions with the "Big Five: Who? What? Where? When? Why?" This alone created an interesting discussion and was a lot more productive than each student simply holding up an item and saying a few words about it. After the "Big Five" Q&A, the first graders who wanted to write about their object were allowed to keep it on their table. Students now had something concrete to write about, and the discussion questions also provided them with rich, descriptive language to add to their writing. One ELL brought a lizard she made out of beads. She wrote a description that day and proudly displayed the item by her writing journal.

BACKPACKS

Thanks goes to my friend and colleague, Merri Gamboa, for another idea to encourage descriptive writing with details. She made a guessing game to link student backpacks to their written descriptions:

1. Do a mini-lesson brainstorming words to describe backpacks: colors, patterns, sizes, shapes, zippers etc.

2. Line up students' backpacks at the front of the class for easy visibility.

3. Students write "secret" descriptions of their own backpacks.

4. Teacher reads each description aloud (one at a time), and the class has to identify the backpack described.

5. Since time may be limited, the "Big Reveals" can take place over several days.

DESCRIBE A CLASSMATE

First graders enjoy using details to describe a classmate. Before we do the activity, I make sure students know appropriate ways (in other words: no unkind descriptions) to describe each other. I set up a simple method to choose the student and to keep it fair:

1. I show large plastic cups labeled #1 and #2.

2. Inside Cup #1 are sticks (craft sticks, or tongue depressors from the school nurse) with student names written on them (one name per stick). Cup #2 is empty; I explain this is where they will put their stick when they are done writing.

Names on sticks are in Cup #1.

3. To model, I call on a student to draw a stick. He picks the stick with a classmate's name.

4. The class brainstorms, and I chart the ways to describe the classmate.

5. Those who are ready to try it, choose their stick right then. (Each child chooses only one stick.)

6. They know to put their stick in Cup #2 when they are done.

7. The cup stays out and available until everyone has had a turn.

8. I know everyone has had a turn when all sticks have moved from Cup #1 to Cup #2. Note: After reading descriptions during conference time, you may want to read some of the descriptions aloud. Or, you may opt to have some students read their writing in Author's Chair, and have the class guess which student is being described.

Extension: This same numbered-cups method can be used early in the year in a Writing Center to invite students to write compliments about each other, or it can be used near the end of the year to have students interview and write about their classmates.

OPPORTUNE MOMENTS

I am always looking for moments that lend themselves to descriptive writing and better word choice over time. Look for people, animals, and events that can naturally involve your class in writing follow-up lessons.

Special Visitor

My teaching partner's husband is a policeman, and his work partner is a German shepherd named Ivan.

In anticipation of his visit to our classroom, we brainstormed in a mini-lesson some details to look for that would describe Ivan. After he left, many students eagerly wrote about the police dog with a badge on his collar. Jennifer was first to share on the projector, and the class helped her circle adjectives and nouns that made a picture in our minds.

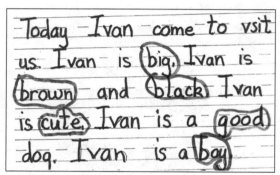

Jennifer's description of Ivan was used in a mini-lesson the next day.

Ivan's visit!

Teacher Observation

Our principal, Mr. Janis, came to our room for *my* teacher observation, but we observed him instead! Turn the tables on your principal to work on word choice and details. I told the students to observe Mr. Janis and describe him, and that afterwards we would make him a character in a story. Here's how the mini-lesson went:

1. I told the class that we were observing Mr. Janis today. As he walked around the room, we brainstormed what he looks like and acts like. (Remind students about appropriate descriptions.)

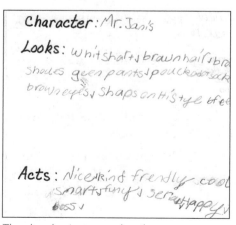

The class brainstorms details.

2. Students first took their own notes on a form I prepared with the headers: "Character: Mr. Janis"; "Looks"; and "Acts." Normally, I might simply have students copy these headers in their journals, but I made the extra effort because the principal was coming! I suggested that when they observe, they should look very carefully to get the details of his hair color, eye color, and clothes. I also prompted for them to add notes about how he acts as a principal.

3. We came together as a group and combined our descriptive words. As I compiled their words on the projector, students could add details they had not thought of to make their notes more complete. If they already had a word down, they put a check mark after it.

4. After this mini-lesson, first graders were encouraged to write a story with Mr. Janis as a character.

KEY WORDS

Occasionally I do mini-lessons on word choice using "Key Words." I collect key chains with simple objects (a soccer ball, a sea otter, a rabbit, a penguin, etc.). Key chains are everywhere—from grocery stores to places I travel. If you can't find a key chain with the specific object you want, use photo key chains (available at craft stores). You can insert a small picture of your topic of study.

When we are studying a new topic, we will brainstorm a word bank of "key words" to go with the unit. I write the words on 3" x 5" index cards. If I have a key chain, I hole punch the index cards and hook them on the ring in advance. During Writing Workshop, first graders can use the key chain with the key words as a springboard for writing.

I spread mini-lessons about adding details with word choice throughout the year. First graders are ready to take on word choice in small doses with many opportunities to try it out. I continue to model writing with both wonderful and boring words. Eventually, the students get savvy and give me an honest evaluation (a unanimous "thumbs down"!) when I deserve it for poor choices that don't spark the reader's imagination.

In place of a child's picture, you can also slip in clip art of any topic— an otter, a whale, a historical figure, etc.

Whales

Whales with baleen eat krill. Humpback whales are as big a bus. They have blubber to keep warm. They have to live in salt water or they'll die out. They breach to give a messy. The whales tail waves bye-bye. Whales are mammals. Whales are not fish. Whales migrate. Whales have a nose on their head

Key words informed this writing on whales.

Using Literature as Writing Models

Mini-lessons using quality literature are always a great model for writing. Well-written text gives me the opportunity to think aloud for a brief, focused lesson. I can pause or reread a segment and talk with the class about wonderful words, intriguing ideas, clear organization, or other elements of the craft of writing. We enjoy the stories or informational text from the point of view of fellow writers.

Here are some of my favorites:

Leads
Ira Says Goodbye by Bernard Waber

Details
Skippyjon Jones series by Judy Schachner

Organization
If You Give a Mouse a Cookie and others in the "If You Give…" series by Laura Numeroff
Edward and the Pirates, by David McPhail
The Important Book by Margaret Wise Brown
Fortunately Unfortunately by Remy Charlip

Problem/Solution
Nate the Great series by Marjorie Weinman Sharmat
Cam Jansen Mysteries by David Adler

Point of View
True Story of the 3 Little Pigs by Jon Scieszka
The Three Little Wolves and the Big Bad Pig by Eugene Trivizas
Somebody and the Three Blairs by Marilyn Tolhurst
Deep in the Forest (wordless) by Brinton Turkle

Read-Aloud Format for Mini-Lessons

1. While reading a section, reread or return to a page from the book to illustrate the point: setting, character description, word choice, organization, etc.

2. Model this target skill on chart paper or on the projector with your own writing.

3. Remind students to try this in their own writing.

4. Conference with students with this skill in mind (other points will also arise).

5. Author's Chair: Have a few students share who tried using the skill in their writing.

Setting

*The Three Little Hawaiian Pigs and
    the Magic Shark* by Donivee M. Laird
The Three Little Javelinas by Susan Lowell
Snow White in New York by Fiona French
Charlotte's Web by E.B. White

Voice

Hey, Little Ant by Phillip and
    Hannah Hoose
Hooway for Wodney Wat by Helen Lester
Night in the Country by Cynthia Rylant
Too Much Noise by Ann McGovern

Word Choice

Click, Clack, Moo: Cows That Type
    by Doreen Cronin
Double Trouble in Walla Walla by
    Andrew Clements
Fancy Nancy series by Jane O'Connor
    and Robin Preiss Glasser
Max's Words by Kate Banks
Miss Alaineus: A Vocabulary Disaster
    by Debra Frasier

Cindiral Gows to Dizinland.
One day a Gril went to Dizinland for a vackichen when she meat a man that sowled [stole] her hart from thi momint she sall [saw] him. cindiral was vasanadet [fascinated] with him. he Got Joumped. cindiral tock him home. he Became part of her life. thay Became mared thay hab 2 kids of thar oun cindiral in the man lived happly every after ps. she is working at can you Blev that she is working at Dizin[

Setting twist: "Cinderella goes to Disneyland."

LITERATURE WITH A TWIST

There are many familiar stories that first graders have heard many times. The story structure of *The Three Little Pigs, Goldilocks and the Three Bears, Three Billy Goats Gruff, Snow White and the Seven Dwarfs,* and others gives a well established oral organization for writing. Make sure to read several of the traditional versions of a tale before having students give a tale a new twist. Following are some ideas on new twists for setting and point of view.

Setting

Creating a new setting for a well known tale is a stretch for some first graders but a welcome challenge for others. I try to balance mini-lessons throughout the year to meet the needs of the spectrum of writers each year. Modeling a change of setting during a shared writing was a lot of fun when we put the "three little pigs" at the big lake about half an hour away. The setting for a twist should be something familiar to your class. A lake setting provided opportunities for a problem with a local coyote—no wolves live in our area. I encourage students to think of places they knew really well so that the setting could be well described and characters changed to fit. One student's story found the pigs living in the desert. When Sarah went to Disneyland, she was eager to use that setting for Cinderella. You can hear the voice of a budding romance writer: "When she met a man who stole her heart from the moment she saw him."

Point of View

Popular children's authors have twisted familiar tales by changing the point of view from the three pigs to the wolf, or from Goldilocks to the three bears. Some first graders will give it a try after just a few encouraging mini-lessons. During a shared writing, we practiced with a story told by the wolf (from *Little Red Riding Hood*), and then some students gave it a go. When those students shared their works in progress, it encouraged others to try a new twist. Anthony had a more realistic ending to his tale of the Three Bears, and he added a sense of drama: "At that very moment, they were in bed."

Flip the Plot

The classic stories, *Alexander and the Terrible, Horrible, No Good, Very Bad Day* and *Alexander, Who Used to Be Rich Last Sunday* by Judith Viorst, are perfect for changing the plot. Students can become the main character and change the events to be the opposite of poor Alexander. "I went to sleep with gum in my mouth and now there's gum in my hair, and when I got out of bed this morning I tripped on the skateboard, and by mistake I dropped my sweater in the sink while the water was running, and I could tell it was going to be a terrible, horrible, no good, very bad day." Then we listed ways to make it a good day (or ways to become rich, when we used *Alexander, Who Used to Be Rich Last Sunday*). Creating a unique plot is hard for many first graders, but changing one that is known is a scaffold many can use.

Here are some other possible well known stories for "Flip the Plot":

When Sophie Gets Angry … by Molly Bang, 1999. When Sophie gets angry, she goes outside and runs, cries, climbs her favorite tree—and then, calmed by the breeze, she is soon ready to go back home." Caldecott Honor Book.
Plot Change: When [name of student]_____feels *happy*, he/she ….

The Relatives Came by Cynthia Rylant, 1985; 2001. Relatives come to visit from Virginia and everyone has a wonderful time. Caldecott Honor Book.
Plot Change: Make the visit a funny disaster.

Where the Wild Things Are by Maurice Sendak, 1963; 1991. After he is sent to bed without supper for behaving like a wild thing, Max dreams of a voyage to the island where the wild things are. Caldecott Award Winner.
Plot Change: A first grader who is good and has happy dreams.

The Snowy Day by Ezra Jack Keats, 1962. The adventures of a little boy in the city on a very snowy day. Caldecott Award Winner.
Plot Change: Tell about the adventures of a first grader in the country on a very sunny summer day.

The wonderful, terrific, Fantasic, very good day

This morning my mom made me brefist. I could tell it was going to be a wondeful, terrific, Fantasic, Very good day. When I got to school I got an A on one of my Paper's.

Unlike "Alexander," Emily decided to have a "wonderful, terrific, fantastic, very good day."

RESPONSE TO LITERATURE

Throughout first grade, I assign a variety of written responses to literature. Most often, this is done daily with the reading in our core program or small-group guided reading. But once in a while, I will do a mini-lesson during Writing Workshop to try a new style of writing.

There were 12 cookies and 12 kids. But 12 more kids came. But there were no more cookies so thay cut it in hafe and thay all got hafe of the cookies.

Andreas's diplomatic new ending…

6 kids were at the door. Bell ranging and they didine open it.

…and Kobe's more realistic one

Change the Ending

The Doorbell Rang by Pat Hutchins is a popular story with first graders who are learning how to share. The two kids in the story have 12 cookies to share until more friends keep ringing the doorbell. Soon, there are 12 kids for the 12 cookies…and the doorbell rings again. Happy ending: It is Grandma with more cookies.

I read the book and then talk about writing to change the ending. "What if Grandma wasn't at the door but it was more hungry friends. How would that ending be?" This creative rewrite brings out the personalities in the class: We have a diplomat and a realist!

Writing a Letter

In the Arnold Lobel book, the chapter "A Lost Button" presents a problem that is not solved in the story. Toad loses a button, and his good friend Frog tries to help. The problem isn't just the lost button but Toad's rude behavior as he gets impatient with his patient friend. The button is found, but has Toad lost his best friend? We chart the rude phrases Toad uses and practice acting out the phrases with a tone of voice that shows impatience and grouchiness. (This is something the kids really get into!) Then to our brainstorming chart, the class adds phrases that Toad can use in his apology. This mini-lesson concludes with an early-writing "friendly letter" format that is actually an apology from Toad to Frog.

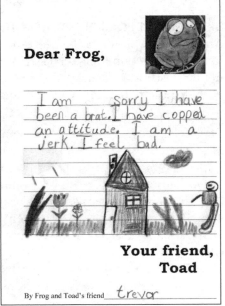

Dear Frog,

I am sorry I have been a brat. I have copped an attitude. I am a jerk. I feel bad.

Your friend, Toad

By Frog and Toad's friend trevor

Trevor gets creative with his "mea culpa."

Writing Fiction: Knowing What's Real and What's Fake

We know that Reading standards expect students to distinguish fiction and nonfiction texts. "Describe characters, settings, and major events in a story, using key details" (CCSS.ELA-Literacy.RL.1.3). This amounts to the necessity for massive exposure to reading and writing, and discussing both throughout the year. Studying text structures gives our first graders the organization to succeed in both reading and writing fiction. To keep it simple for six-year-olds, I help them remember the word *fiction* by linking it to "fake." They can usually tell when something is pretend, such as animals talking, or time travelling, or other clearly unrealistic elements. I remind them that these stories are fake; they are fiction. Realistic fiction, however, can be a bit more subtle and becomes a topic for the end of the year. Here are a few mini-lessons to scaffold this important next step as they move away from stories only about themselves.

SORT FICTION AND NONFICTION BOOKS

Common Core State Standards expect our first graders to "Explain major differences between books that tell stories and books that give information, drawing on a range of text types" (CCSS.ELA-Literacy.RL.1.5). Early in first grade, I make a chart for us to list our read-alouds and categorize them as Fake/Fiction or Real/Nonfiction. This list builds over time so that the elements of a story (characters/setting/problem/events/solution) and informational texts (information/facts/text features) become apparent. Every time we start a new unit of study in Science or Social Studies, I do the same. We look at books about George Washington in February and sort the ones with facts from those that are fiction. A great fiction book for first grade is *George Washington's Socks* by Elvira Woodruff: *A mysterious rowboat transports five adventurous kids back in time to the eve of the Battle at Trenton where they experience the American Revolution.* Time travel? Yup, that's fake!

BRAINSTORM POSSIBLE FICTION TOPICS

After we have sorted books and talked about the different structures in them, it is time to chart the fiction topics. This chart serves as a reference for the variety of ways to craft fiction. List 10-15 popular fiction books/series you have shared so far in first grade. After each, list the fiction topic/plot. It might look something like this:

Amanda Pig, First Grader	a pig goes to school
Clifford the Big Red Dog	giant dog has adventures
Mrs. Wishy Washy	farm animals talk
Skippyjon Jones	talking cat thinks he is a Chihuahua
Arthur Series	animal characters have problems at home and school
The Very Hungry Caterpillar	a caterpillar eats so much food he gets a tummy ache
Junie B. Jones Series	a made-up girl gets in trouble at school and home
Miss Nelson Is Missing	a scary made-up substitute is hired
Cat in the Hat	a talking cat causes trouble
The Three Little Pigs	talking pigs live in people-like houses
Magic Tree House Series	Kids time-travel to the past for adventures

MODEL WRITING A PIECE OF FICTION

Before looking at the story structure of fiction, I model writing a quick story and think aloud as I make it up.

Using the names of teachers, principals, and students engages the class in the process. Students think it is hilarious that the aliens stole our jump ropes. In sharing that day, more models of fiction are shared, and we emphasize the pretend elements in our discussion. Soon enough, some students are ready to give fiction writing a try. Misty shares a moose story that seems like it could be informational text, and the class analyzes why it is fiction.

Later, Bobby gets everyone's creative juices flowing with his dragon and flying saucer battle story. Now everyone wants to try making up a story! As crucial as my modeled writing is, student work is a catalyst for having a go at something new.

Writing a short, imaginary story on the overhead

A blue moose? That's unreal!

STORY-PLANNING GRAPHIC ORGANIZER

The graphic organizer based on story structure (Reproducible 14) is used for many mini-lessons over the course of the year. Each lesson follows the "Brainstorm/Model/Try It/Share It" format, and these components are given as individual mini-lessons before they are used as a whole: characters, setting, events, problem/solution. We also discuss that stories have a beginning, middle, and an ending. There are generally no step-by-step procedures for these mini-lessons; we simply discuss, brainstorm ideas, and whenever possible, practice writing.

Mini-Lesson: Characters

We practice descriptive writing about how characters might look and how they might act. With some gentle pushing, first graders can understand that characters can act like people they may know: *smart, funny, bossy, know-it-all, shy,* etc. We make up the labels and then chart what that shy, or bossy person, for instance, would say and do.

Mini-Lesson: Setting—Where and When?

Places are fun to brainstorm—from the exotic (outer space) to the local (playground). We create and post a chart of possible locations, and then make another one for temporal words. Working a "when" word into writing at this early level is more of a challenge because it is not as visually concrete as a place. Here are some temporal concepts to talk about and include.

day/week/month/year

yesterday/today/tomorrow

prepositions that can be used to describe the position and sequence of an event in time

after	before	between	by
during	following	for	from
on	since	to	until

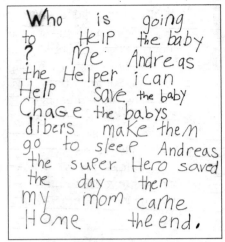

This superhero changes diapers and puts a baby to sleep!

Mini-Lesson: Events

We will work more on events when we are working on organization, but a good start for writing is to plan three different events for the characters. After pointing this out and briefly discussing it, Andreas declares himself a superhero and tells the ways he saves the new baby before Mom comes home.

Mini-Lesson: Problems

It is time to think of some significant problems, issues, or adventures that we can use in our pretend stories. First graders come up with a host of potential problems from the fantastic (kooky, messy aliens hide in our garage and won't leave) to the more realistic (a friend got a new neighbor and doesn't have time for me anymore). We brainstorm some ideas and add them to a Problem/Solution chart. We validate that making up a pretend fight with a friend is just as worthy as a volcano eruption with a helicopter rescue.

Mini-Lesson: Solutions

Solutions are essential. Otherwise the characters are left in dire straits. For mini-lessons on solutions to problems, I prefer to use student work that needs a more fully-developed solution. With their permission, I share their work on the projector or interactive whiteboard, or I have them read their work to a group. Classmates are eager to give suggestions to solve the problem completely. Like endings, this part of writing fiction will continue to develop throughout the grades. I believe we plant important seeds with Writing Workshop in first grade.

Together we look at some of the problems, both realistic and far-fetched, and then come up with some solutions to those problems. The result is a Problem/Solution chart that is displayed in the classroom to serve as a reference for future fiction writing.

Mini-Lesson: Endings

Typically with first grade writing, stories just stop suddenly, or students abruptly slap on "The End." Not much finesse or closure goes into ending these stories! I do lots of modeling on how to write endings, and work on this is often a subject of conferencing before publication. The truth is... learning how to craft a good ending to a fiction piece starts in first grade but develops more fully in the later grades.

Writing Nonfiction to Support Science & Social Studies

Naturally, I will have the class write about our Science and Social Studies curriculum topics. Science and Social Studies are essential aspects of our curriculum, and thus are perfect topics for our forays into nonfiction writing. Of course, we teachers know there are even more chances every week to write informational texts. First graders drag in all their "treasures" (rocks, seashells, feathers, flowers, creatures, etc.). I put them in a place where they can be admired and stimulate writing. However, when the leaves and shells and plastic dinosaurs start piling up, it is definitely time to brainstorm words and methods to use in nonfiction writing.

Our brainstorming chart about fall leaves

KEY WORDS FOR NONFICTION

Carlos brought in his pet mouse Puffball for a visit. In questioning the proud owner, we learned that the mouse had a wheel but wasn't very good at "driving" it. The class knows we will brainstorm key words for writing, and whenever we do, I put these words on a small whiteboard that is positioned near our topic of study. In this case, our list was next to Puffball's cage. We do this brainstorming mini-lesson the same way we did the "Key Words" activity (see page 71), but because we explore different nonfiction topics at different times— that coincide with our Science and Social Studies units— it makes more sense to post charts of content-area vocabulary at the times when we are focused on those topics. For example, Puffball was visiting the class for a limited time, so we put Puffall and a word list together in a specific area. Morgan and others wanted to write about Puffball, so they took turns looking closely at the mouse and the list of key words.

Actual leaves stimulate writing about this Science topic.

MODEL TEXT STRUCTURES WITH THINK-ALOUDS

Throughout first grade, we work on reading and writing nonfiction texts. They certainly go hand in hand because reading is a model for our writing. One of our goals in Writing Workshop is that first graders will "write informative/explanatory texts in which they name a topic, supply some facts about the topic, and provide some sense of closure" (CCSS.ELA-Literacy.W.1.2). Thinking aloud as we look at text structures unique to informational texts makes the difference between fiction and nonfiction transparent. Kids get it when we dramatically look at a gorgeous dinosaur book with photographs of dinosaur skeletons (*The Dinosaur*

Carlos has a mouse in a mouse house. It has a ball. He's a bad driver. He eats corn and seeds. He drank with his bottolle.

A student writes about Puffball while he is visiting in the classroom.

Museum: An Unforgettable, Virtual Interactive Tour Through Dinosaur History by National Geographic Society). I put it to the students: "Do we see fake characters here or real dinosaur bones?" Then I pull out *Patrick's Dinosaurs* by Carol Carrick, and we look at the illustrations of Patrick's imagined dinosaurs, and his town and house as he walks home from school. "Could this be real, or does Patrick have a wonderful imagination?" I ask, "Why?" I take students deeper with my think-alouds when the nonfiction book has illustrations rather than photographs. I also have to get students into the text: "Is there information to learn or a good story with characters and a setting?" In your own classroom, whatever you are studying at the time in Science or Social Studies will work fine for this comparison. You can also consider the nonfiction companions that are now part of the Magic Tree House series. If the major nonfiction text structures come up naturally in a book we are using, I will mention them informally: *Description or a List; Sequence or Time Order; Compare and Contrast; Cause and Effect; Problem and Solution*.

NONFICTION TEXT FEATURES

The basic structure of nonfiction is to convey information. Unique to this structure are the text features the author and illustrator may use. It is important to call attention to and teach these in Reading and Read-Alouds before we can expect young writers to take on the challenge of understanding them in their own reading and using them in their own writing. The Common Core State Standards in Reading Informational Texts state that students should: "Know and use various text features (e.g., headings, table of contents, glossaries, electronic menus, icons) to locate key facts or information in a text" (CCSS. ELA-Literacy.RI.1.5). A nonfiction book may include these features, as well as diagrams, maps, photographs, and captions. Here are my first grade-friendly definitions:

Table of Contents: a page in the front of a book with major headings/topics and starting pages

Heading: the title of a section that tells me what that part is about

Glossary: an ABC list of the important words and their meaning for this book

Index: a detailed list of topics at back of the book, with pages to find the information

Caption: words that help me understand a picture or diagram

Diagram: a drawing that labels the parts of something

Map: a drawing of places that help me know where something is located

Photograph: photos that help me see what the topic looks like in real life

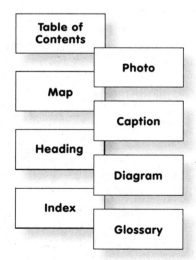

Some Nonfiction Text Features cards

I make and keep "Nonfiction Text Features" cards handy to use for reading and writing informational texts. In the past, I would just mention the photograph or glossary or map, but experience has taught me that picking up the card and labeling it makes the connection more concrete for first graders. Again, you can make your own cards using index cards or by writing out the terms and photocopying onto cardstock.

Over time, they will have many examples of such text features to label from our Science and Social Studies guided-reading nonfiction books and read-alouds. To get them involved, I make a game of it:

Label It

1. Pull a nonfiction book from the classroom or school library on a topic we are studying, such as "George Washington" or "dinosaurs."

2. Arrange the class into small groups.

3. Display the Nonfiction Text Features cards for all to see. (I use a pocket chart.)

4. Review reading the cards and talking about what they mean.

5. Show a text feature from the chosen book and have students confer quietly in their group:
   I think it is a _____ because _____.

6. As a class, discuss which label fits best and why. Groups who determined the correct label get a star on the board.

7. Repeat #5 with more text features.

8. The group(s) with the most stars gets a simple prize (like lining up first for recess).

Book Detectives

1. Pull nonfiction books from your classroom and/or school library on a topic you are studying, such as the water cycle or insects.

2. Depending on the number of books, arrange students into small groups or partners.

3. Hand out the books.

4. Mix up the Nonfiction Text Features cards in a hat or box, and dramatically pull one out. Review what it means and how it looks in informational texts.

5. "Ready, Set, Go!" The groups look through their book(s) for the text feature.

6. "Time's up!" Time for groups to share what they found and what they learned from the feature.

7. Reflect:
   Do all _____ books have _____? (topic + text feature)
   What did we learn about _____ using _____? (topic + text feature)

FACT FINDING

Finding factual information in books and then writing that information can be a challenge for some first graders who might not know much about the topic. Here are some fun ways to get young writers started on an informational writing project.

Tip

I model writing what I learned about the topic and what additional information the text feature provided. For example, I define the feature (Table of Contents) and make a list of the important things I can find out about George Washington using the TOC.

I will also frequently model a "quick write" on the topic and create that text feature to add information. For example, I might describe a Monarch Butterfly, then draw a diagram and label the body parts.

Start Simple: "3 Facts"

When we studied Abraham Lincoln with various books, we created a word bank (of facts) to use in our writing. We then chose three facts from our word bank to start writing our nonfiction piece about Lincoln. Using just "3 Facts" is a great way to get young writers started in a nonfiction effort.

Mystery Facts

As we continue to work on writing facts, I like to tie it into our current unit of Science or Social Studies. When we were studying the rainforest and the animals that live there, we created a "mystery" with facts as clues.

1. Each student "secretly" decided on an animal to study that lives in the rainforest.

2. Privately, they told me, and I wrote it down.

3. We researched the animal using the Internet and library books. This activity is yet another connection to the standards: "Participate in shared research and writing projects" (CCSS.ELA-Literacy.W.1.7).

4. Notes are taken and later written into simple clues that describe the habitat and the animal. Early in the year, upper-grade buddies write the notes on scrap paper from "I learned" statements the first graders dictate. Later, the buddies serve as readers and first graders can write simple "I learned" statements in their writing journals.

Tip

This is a good time to have upper-grade buddies help. They can read the text to your first graders (in small portions), then ask, "What did you learn?"

5. First graders write at least three clues on one side of a sheet of paper and draw the animal on the back with its name for the "big reveal."

6. One by one, over several days, writers share in Author's Chair and then entertain guesses from their audience.

NOTE: This is a fun activity to keep for Open House in the spring. As part of the class tour, Enasia read her facts to see if her family knew the answer. . . *jaguar*!

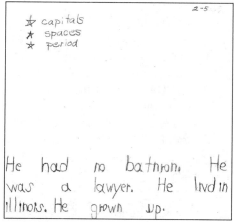

Aleks used our word bank to find "3 facts" for his writing about Abraham Lincoln: lawyer, Illinois, grown.

Mystery Writing: turning facts into clues

The "big reveal" on the back of the page

FACT OR OPINION?

First graders have been writing facts for a while but need work on separating factual information (*They can run 30 mph.*) from opinion (*They are cute.*). The first standard for writing in the Common Core State Standards expects students to learn how to "Write opinion pieces in which they introduce the topic. . . state an opinion, supply a reason for the opinion, and provide some sense of closure" (CCSS.ELA-Literacy.W.1.1).

I do several mini-lessons where I write statements that are clearly true/verifiable in books or online, and others that are clearly my own (wild) opinions. I start with a fact and then add an "I think..." statement to show the difference when it is my opinion. I encourage students give it a try, and those who try it either share in Author's Chair or have their work featured in upcoming mini-lessons. Lexus used both facts and opinions in her writing, and the class sorted them out sentence by sentence.

When we started our spring study of silkworms, we brainstormed words to write about their life cycle. Our brainstorming chart had two columns: *Facts* and *Opinions*.

> It is vary Cloudy. I think it going to rain. It is windy. I think wer going to have a storm. It is foggy. It is over cast a Littel. It is nor sunny.

Fact or Opinion?

> The eggs are yellow. The moth can+t fly. On the coon was the eggs. moths youst to be a Silkworm. The silkworm made a cocon insid the cocon

Silkworm facts by Marina

> They are creepee and crolee. They feel like a lady bug. Silkworms do. They have a dot on the butt. it is werd looking.

Opinions about silkworms by Marina

SIMPLE GRAPHIC ORGANIZER: INFORMATIONAL WRITING

It is extremely helpful to do mini-lessons using a simple graphic organizer for informational writing.

Taking notes on the Simple Graphic Organizer for Informational Writing (Reproducible 15), I model how to turn them into sentences on the projector. We are studying "simple machines" for our class Science Fair Project and practice using the graphic to jot down notes about each machine. Then, using this organizer, Aleks writes sentences around the facts he knows about the screw as a simple machine. The third sentence is copied from a sample I wrote to model a sentence; the others Aleks wrote on his own. Aleks is an excellent example of the progress an ELL can make with daily writing. Seven months earlier, he came into first grade speaking no English and only drawing pictures for his writing.

GRAPHIC ORGANIZER WITH DETAILS: INFORMATIONAL WRITING

The next step in meeting the standards pushes first graders further in the craft of writing: "With guidance and support from adults, focus on a topic, respond to questions and suggestions from peers, and add details to strengthen writing as needed (CCSS.ELA-Literacy.W.1.5). TayBrieja is typical of most developing writers who become adept at facts but lack details. I can conference with her to get elaboration on whales ("support from adults"), but can also use her writing as a mini-lesson the next day to get "questions and suggestions from peers." I listen to first graders ask TayBrieja many of the questions I would have asked, and I fill out a new graphic organizer that links facts to details for her. (Reproducible 16) We will go over this organizer together in a conference.

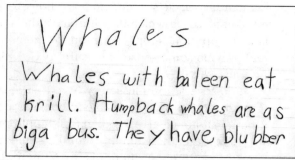

Even good informational writing, like TayBreija's on whales, can lack supporting details.

Since the class has been doing a study of whales, students are eager to ask questions and give comments and compliments:

"Can you tell how baleen is like a toothbrush?"

"People outside our class might not know what krill is."

"I like the way you said 'big as a bus,' not just *big*."

Writing nonfiction texts to inform an audience is not an overnight or even two-week process. I weave it in throughout the year, doing mini-lessons that follow the class. We are meeting standards and strengthening the reciprocal reading/writing process. Sometimes it feels like baby steps, but I see progress, for instance, when Marina writes about spider legs and includes the number of legs, and when Trevor writes about pandas and uses "because" to add a detail.

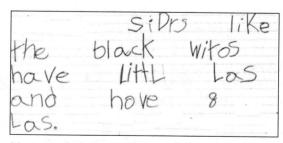

Marina includes a detail about the number of legs a spider has.

Trevor states a fact and gives a supporting detail.

Organization

Organizing first grade writing is a major goal: "Write narratives in which they recount two or more appropriately sequenced events, include some details regarding what happened, use temporal words to signal event order, and provide some sense of closure" (CCSS.ELA-Literacy.W.1.3). With six- and seven-year-olds sequential organization is done over time and in scaffolded steps.

LEARNING TEMPORAL WORDS FOR ORGANIZATION

Before first graders can be expected to write using temporal words, I believe they need massive oral practice and opportunities to learn and practice the words in a variety of contexts. I create word cards for them, and we learn them by acting them out and using them in a variety of school contexts. (Again, to create your own cards, use standard index cards or copy terms onto cardstock.) Early in the year, I may focus on just three basic transition words—*first, next, last*—and eventually work in *then* and *finally*. There are also many opportunities at school to practice organization using ordinal number words—*first, second, third, fourth*, etc.:

Lining up to go to lunch: "Which group will line up <u>first</u>?"

Turning in books in the library: "Sarah's table will go <u>next</u>."

Sequencing a story in a guided-reading group: "<u>First</u> the cow jumped in the mud…"

Doing an art project: "For the <u>third</u> step, we…"

Making a gingerbread house: "<u>Finally</u>, wrap your project to go home"

During a science experiment on incline planes:

<u>First</u>, the car rolled slowly on the flat board.

<u>Then</u>, Anthony made the incline plane with the block.

<u>Last</u>, the car rolled quickly down the incline plane.

Act It Out—Again

We saw that a great way to learn a classroom procedure is to "Act It Out" (Chapter 2). This method works when learning temporal words, too. Acting something out lets first graders see it, hear it, and do it—and this helps make the learning stick. I use P.E. class to do mini-lessons that use all modalities: *visual, auditory,* and *kinesthetic*. In advance of the mini-lesson, label index cards with the temporal words you are targeting. In this case, I labeled cards: *First, Next, Then, Finally*.

1. Take the class outside and take the word cards you might need.

2. Choose 2–4 students to play a brief game.

3. Lead the class in sequencing what happened. Here is what we did with 2 students playing basketball:

Agree on what happened *first*; give a student that card to hold up when we say it. Everyone repeats what happened *first:*

"*First*, Alex took the basketball out to recess."

Discuss what happened *next*; give a student that card to hold up when we say it. Everyone repeats what happened *first* and *next:*

Next, *Richard took a shot.*

Then, *Alex chased the ball.*

Finally, *they lined up when the bell rang.*

"*First*, Alex took the basketball out to recess."

"*Next*, Richard took a shot."

Talk about what happened *then*; give a student that card to hold up when we say it.
   Everyone repeats what happened *first, next*, and *then*:

"*First*, Alex took the basketball out to recess."

"*Next*, Richard took a shot."

"*Then*, Alex chased the ball."

Agree what *finally* happened; give a student that card to hold up when we say it.
   Everyone repeats what happened *first, next, then,* and *finally*:

"*First*, Alex took the basketball out to recess."

"*Next*, Richard took a shot."

"*Then*, Alex chased the ball."

"*Finally*, they lined up when the bell rang"

4. If time allows, you can repeat with new kids acting it out and holding the cards. Everyone always repeats the words.

5. Other topics for sequencing might include: *slide, jump rope, soccer, tetherball, tag,* or *hopscotch.*

SEQUENCING IN READING LESSONS

Whether in whole-class core reading lessons or small-group guided reading, the stories we read are perfect material for mini-lessons on sequencing. Even before using the word cards, I can start simply by having students number sentences as they put a story in order.

However, this is only a temporary scaffold until I introduce the word cards. (Using the word cards as labels allows us to tell what happened in ordinal numerical order.) Mini-lessons will include shared writing using a core literature story:

Materials:
- story the class is currently reading
- sentence strips
- pocket chart
- Ordinal Number word cards

First Grade Writing Workshop © 2014 Judy Lynch • Scholastic Teaching Resources

How:

1. Discuss the big events in the story.

2. Teacher writes them on sentence strips, and the class reads each one.

3. Mix up the sentence strips.

4. Reorder them into sequence, rechecking in the story. Reread.

5. Place the ordinal word cards with each sentence in the pocket chart and reread with the words, *first, second, third*, etc.

> 1. They had to get out fas
> 2. the water get in the haws.
> 3. the Phone wus dead
> 4. the Water wus drtey,
> 5. Andy cam to hlpe Them.
>
> 6. They Prot Sum to yss.

Early sequencing activities using literature: Students number sentences in order.

What have we done? Massive amounts or reading and thinking about the order of the story as we write and manipulate the text in the pocket chart. This activity is a support for writing, but it also teaches summarization in first grade reading.

PERSONAL-PICTURES SEQUENCING

With Personal-Pictures Sequencing, we are learning the craft of writing a personal narrative and how to organize a *beginning, middle,* and *end*. (As above, create cards using standard index cards or by copying terms onto cardstock.)

Materials:
3 pages in their journals
Beginning, Middle, End cards

How:

DAY 1:

1. I model with the word cards (*Beginning/Middle/End*) the three main things I did at recess. I label the top of three pages in my journal: *Beginning, Middle, End*
I draw a picture at the top of one journal page of Dulce with her coat on.
I draw a picture of Mr. McLaughlin our principal on the next page.
I draw a picture of a cell phone to remind me I called Mr. Lynch on the third page

2. I think out loud how the pictures and labels will help me write about the beginning, middle, and end of my recess. Then I add the text to each page:
I helped Dulce with her coat. The zipper was stuck. She said, "Thank you," and then went out to recess.
I talked to Mr. McLaughlin in the office. I was checking to see if our field trip to the zoo was approved. He said "Yes," so all the first grade teachers were excited.
I had a little time left before the bell, so I called Mr. Lynch to see what time he would be home from practice tonight. He said spring football practice would be done about 5 o'clock.

DAY 2:

3. I remind the class to pay attention to three things they do at recess. I show them my pictures and writing from the previous day about the beginning, middle and end of my recess. They know that we will all do the labels, three drawings, and writing after recess.

Every once in awhile, the entire class will all do the same type of writing together (though they still choose what to write about within the skill of "organization.") If students are not finished with a previous piece, I show them how to skip several pages in their journals to allow room so they can go back to it later.

4. Labels: Once back in class, I lead students in labeling the tops of three pages in their journals: *Beginning, Middle, End.*

5. Pictures: I model partner sharing with a student, who points to each page and tells me what he or she will draw in detail.

6. Partners share the details they will put into their beginning, middle, and end pictures.

7. Each student draws their three pictures. I conference with my ELLs who need extra support.

8. For closure, I put students with new partners; they point to each picture and discuss what they will write tomorrow in detail.

Telling the exact order of losing a tooth is important to first graders with mouths full of holes.

DAY 3+:

9. Writing: Over the next several days, students create personal narratives and share in Author's Chair as they finish.

Later, Bobby was eager to share his second recess story about snails on the playground. He wanted to show off page numbers we had talked about in a conference as the next step after word labels.

Organization with temporal words gives a mental and visual structure for first grade writing. It lays a foundation that will help them organize their writing in the next few grades. I smile when first graders use temporal and transitional words. I smile even bigger when their writing shows good organization without heavy scaffolding. Eventually, organization is evident even without temporal words.

ORGANIZE WRITING WITH "HOW-TO'S"

The Common Core Standards expect us to provide opportunities throughout the year for students to "participate in shared research and writing projects, for example, explore a number of "how-to" books on a given topic and use them to write a sequence of instructions (CCSS.ELA-Literacy.W.1.7). The temporal words we have been using are crucial to step-by-step directions. To start the year, I do shared writing mini-lessons with very simple directions for:

How to take turns on the slide

How to tie your shoe

How to come to the rug for Author's Chair

How to sharpen a pencil

How to make a sandwich

How to build a snowman

I look for books to read aloud that give directions or steps as a model for writing.

Building a House by Byron Barton

Garbage Trucks at Work by D. R. Addison

How Did That Get in My Lunchbox: The Story of Food by Chris Butterworth

How to Draw People by Barbara Levy

Simple Machines (Starting With Science) by Deborah Hodge

The Post Office Book: Mail and How It Moves by Gail Gibbons

The Usborne Book of Face Painting by Chris Chaudron

The Ultimate Book of Kid Concoctions by John E. Thomas

Transformed: How Everyday Things Are Made by Bill Slavin

Sometimes a student will spontaneously want to give directions. On yard duty one morning, I noticed Jackson had a group admiring his new curly hair. I asked about it, and he gave us step-by-step information about how he got his new "do." In Writing Workshop that day, I nonchalantly said, "I think some of us forgot how to do the curls. Can you write it down for all of us?" He dove into it and amused us all in Author's Chair with the piece titled "How to Remove Your Stupid Hairdos."

If students are stuck in a rut of writing the same thing over and over, conferencing can encourage something new such as "How-To" pieces. When I told Jonathon I didn't know how to play Nintendo, he gladly gave me directions. After Jonathon shared in Author's Chair, an eager group wanted to tell me how to play their favorite games. I simply said, "Write good directions. And because this is all new to me, I'll need them in exact order." The temporal words are put to use again.

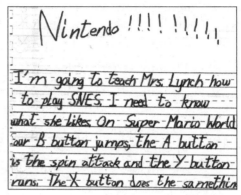

Teaching Mrs. Lynch how to play SNES

ORGANIZE WRITING WITH LETTERS

Writing "friendly" letters is a common skill in standards, and we can easily work that into Writing Workshop. First graders need to learn the format and organization unique of letter writing (e.g., the opening/greeting: *Dear* _____ ; the content/body; the closing: *sincerely, your friend, love,* etc.; the signature). I start the first month of school by modeling simple letters in Writing Workshop, and then having students practice during Writing Center.

Writing Center Practice for Letter Writing

Materials:

5" x 8" index cards for writing post cards to classmates

Mail Box (a shoe box works, but one from the hardware store lets students put up the "flag" when mail is inside)

How:

1. Choose a stick from the Cup #1 to select the person who will get the letter. (Use sticks prepared for "Describe a Classmate," page 69.)

2. Look at the posted sample format.

3. Write a letter and sign it.

4. Put the letter in the mailbox.

5. Put the name stick in Cup #2.

Letter-Writing Station: sticks with student's names and cups labeled "1" and "2"

> February 19,
> Dera Nancy do you.
> wot to be my thrd
> besnt frend I
> wood be (Happy)
> yor best.
> fred

A "friend request"

> Dear Mrs. Gleason's Class,
> Thank you for the silk
> worms. The silk worms
> are nice. They eat
> a lot.
> Love, Anthony

A "Thank You" note

Look for Letter-Writing Opportunities

Throughout the year, I can do mini-lessons when writing opportunities come up. Some I have used in the past include:

Writing letters to friends in other classes

Writing letters of thanks

Writing letters to each new president and governor (and often they write back!)

Writing letters to our buddy class to ask for help on a project

Writing to a character in a book we are reading

Writing to a classmate or staff member who is leaving

Writing letters that ask questions of the principal, the custodian, the librarian, or other interesting members of the community

> Dear Boo, You need to fliy a
> kiet. Then you need a strying. Then
> you need to drol a qichr. Then
> you need to run and run. You
> find a flat qlase.
> Love,
> Chris

A letter to "Boo" after reading Boo Bear Flies a Kite

Organization is the craft of writing that gives structure to our first grade writing. These mini-lessons lay the foundational groundwork for meeting standards in the grades to follow in elementary school. Oh yes, those teachers will be thanking us!

Conferencing: Beyond the First Six Weeks

As usual, after the mini-lesson, I circulate the room, checking in with the class. My good friend Darla Wood-Walters calls this "teaching like an octopus." Checking in here and there, spending time as needed, redirecting, praising, pushing a bit, and taking quick notes on my clipboard. And again, I always look at each student's writing with that lens that Donald Graves showed me:

Following the Child: What does this child know? What does this child need?

As I conference throughout first grade, there is still a range of writing from student to student. Never a dull moment!

First Grade Writing Workshop © 2014 Judy Lynch • Scholastic Teaching Resources

Misty:

What does she know?

I bend down to conference with Misty and admire the details in her illustration. She has gotten immersed in her drawing but says "I don't know what to write."

What does she need?

I take her back to her illustration and ask, "What's happening here?" That's enough to get her chatting about her dog. I repeat her ideas back to her to firm them up in her mind. A quick title, "My Dog," and she is ready to write.

Questioning gave Misty ideas for her writing.

Morgan:

What does she know?

Morgan is a confident writer, and her writing is easy to read with mostly standard spelling, spaces, and punctuation. She is an easy student to overlook because her work looks good. But on closer examination, she has written the typical "bed to bed" story with events in order but no detail.

What does she need?

I compliment Morgan on her retelling of her entire day in order. I tell her I am curious to know if she can focus on a smaller part of the day and give extended details on that. We are thinking about her audience and sharing more of what really happened. I conference with her about picking one part of the day in which she is most interested. She started elaborating on the pancakes. We tried a new journal page, and she titled it "Sunday Pancakes." When she shared this writing in Author's Chair, one student remarked, "You made me hungry!"

A typical "bed to bed" story: events in order but no detail

Conferencing About Topics

By the middle of first grade, the whole class has their own copy of the Topic Chart (see page 65) to refer to when writing. I run them on cardstock, and they are kept in the students' writing folders. At the beginning of the year, we brainstormed topics using a group chart. Now, they get their own chart, and when conferencing, we can add new topics under broad categories typical of first grader's interests.

CONFERENCING WHEN THEY ARE "STUCK"

What do we do when they have hit a wall and can't come up with a topic or they are in a rut writing about the same topic? Here is something that has worked for me:

Format: Brainstorm more topics with the "stuck" student

    Teacher writes the new topics directly into the student's journal
    Student chooses one new topic to write about that day
    Student puts a star or check mark in front of the new topic
    Student commits by writing the title and date into journal

Add topics to their topic chart as you chat:

Tell me more about your:

- family, friends
- pets (make one up if you want to write fiction)
- neighborhood
- birthday (When is it? What are you planning to do?)
- chores you do at home to help
- favorite holiday
- favorite book you've read
- favorite sports/games at recess (Tell me how to play it.)

What kind of writing would you like to try?

What's a story you tell again and again?

What are you good at?

What have you heard/seen/felt that you can't forget?

What would you like to know?

What is a problem at school? How would you solve it?

CONFERENCING TWIST: HELP THEM HELP THEMSELVES

Sometimes it hits me: make them responsible! There are occasionally some first graders who depend on me too much. This classroom is full of writers, so I simply say: "Read three of your friends' stories and get ideas from them."

Other times a first grader is capable of thinking of his or her own topics and may just be craving my attention. I give that student a sticky note to take home and write new topics. Then, I give the student massive attention for being independent when the sticky note comes back with ideas on it. We add the new ideas to his or her journal. The kudos continue when the student shares the sticky note from home and the new story in Author's Chair. Jonathon shows the class the topics he came up with at home independently: *funny ghosts, weird monsters, giants, love stories.*

Jonathon's sticky-note topics

Choosing Topics Independently

My goal is that first graders start choosing their topics independently if and when they are ready. Sometimes they need a conference to bridge the gap between my support and their independence. During conferencing with Sarah, she chooses two possible topics. As a scaffold I write them on a sticky note for her to remember. She decides to write about her trees first.

Periodically, I ask the class to give advice to each other on choosing topics. I post these as a reference point for independence. Lily sums it up well:

You can write about your teacher and school. You can write about roses. You can write about Family. You can write about your DOG! Lily

First Grade Writing Workshop © 2014 Judy Lynch • Scholastic Teaching Resources

HELPING HAND TO PLAN A STORY

Nothing is "handier" for a graphic organizer than a hand with question words for each finger. I introduce this in a mini-lesson and then use it in conferencing as a planner. Eventually, the questions after a first draft move first graders to simple revision.

Foundational Mini-Lesson

Materials:

- *Aunt Isabel Tells a Good One* by Kate Duke (Isabel helps plan a story with question words.)
- Helping Hand graphic
- Large chart (to draw on) or a copy of the Helping Hand chart

How: *Day 1 Teacher Models Planning a Story*
Teacher models for the group how to trace and label their hands.
Teacher models on the projector or chart paper how to plan a story by using
    Who? What? Where? When? Why? and taking notes.
Teacher models how to make a sentence out of each note.

Day 2 Group Plan
Teacher reviews her plan and story from the previous day.
Take the class step by step, finger by finger, through group story plan.
Group decides on a new topic to write about and puts it in the middle of the hand.
Together, they take simple notes with teacher modeling on chart or projector.
Students practice writing on the back of the page.

Day 3 Individual Plan
Students are encouraged to plan their own stories using the Helping Hand.
Blank copies are passed out for each folder and used when needed.
Blank copies are made available in an accessible spot.
Students plan their own stories independently or with teacher conferences
    as needed.
Students write their own stories.
Students who try to use all elements are featured in Author's Chair.

HELPING HAND AS A CONFERENCING TOOL

In conferencing, a range of writers can use the Helping Hand to plan their writing. I can be the scribe, or they write independently. This graphic organizer helps me follow each child and differentiate my conferences.

Kobe

I sit down next to Kobe and ask him to read the sentence he has written.

Kobe's pre-conference writing

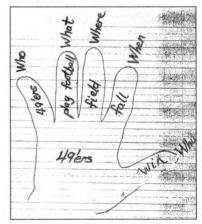

Kobe plans writing with a Helping Hand Chart.

    He shrugs and says simply, "I don't know…" Ah, time to give him some support! I trace his hand and help him plan a new piece. He is a football fan, so I ask him about that. I write his notes on the hand chart while asking him a question for each finger.

I stay with him to model that he can take his note, "49ers", and turn it into a sentence. "What do you want to say about your team?" He confidently writes, "I like the 49ers." I leave him to continue so that he doesn't depend on me for every sentence, but I check back in to see how it's going.

Jonathon

Jonathon is an advanced writer who had slacked off. Noticing the simple writing his classmates produced, he did that for awhile. I conferenced with him about my concern, and I praised his more detailed pieces. I encouraged him to plan his own story with the Helping Hand. Jonathon drew his own Helping Hand chart, and then planned for his next piece of writing. Author's Chair that day featured Jonathon talking about his process. He dazzled his classmates and served as a model for them, too.

Jonathon made a Helping Hand and shared his planning process in Author's Chair.

Conferencing to Improve Sentences

I have to remind myself that formal sentence structure is a convention of written language. What do most children bring to school in Kindergarten? Oral language. Speaking is often just a couple of words or phrases, and this oral language will show up in children's writing. Andreas was excited to write about Bruce Lee and knew a lot about this karate icon. "How do you know so much about Bruce Lee?" I asked. "Mom taught me at home, I kept it in my brain."

Andreas's opening two sentences show voice and capture our attention: *How about Bruce Lee? He died in 1399 before I was born.* Most of his paragraph after that is then written in phrases, almost like notes. I don't want to squelch his enthusiasm (I'll deal with the birth date if this goes to publication), but I do need to address the use of phrases instead of sentences.

> HOW about Bruce
> Lee He died in 1399
> Befor I wes Born.
> Brown Eyes Black Hair
> No shert black pant
> No shoes Knoykr Oty
> His dad dident
> teLL Him to
> fite.   no to use

My conference with Andreas aims at keeping his voice while improving his sentences.

PULL THE WRITING OFF THE PAGE:

First, I praised his hook at the beginning. Then, we looked at the other complete thoughts with a *Who?* and *What happened?* format:

SENTENCE: He died. . . *Who?* Bruce Lee   *What happened?* . . .died before I was born

SENTENCE: Dad. . .   *Who?* His dad   *What happened?* . . .didn't tell him to fight.

Next, we used the format on his phrases, which I wrote separately on a whiteboard. We asked the questions for each phrase to determine a sentence:

No shirt	*Who?*	*What happened?*	No shoes	*Who?*	*What happened?*
black pants	*Who?*	*What happened?*	Knows karate	*Who?*	*What happened?*
brown eyes	*Who?*	*What happened?*	No house	*Who?*	*What happened?*
black hair	*Who?*	*What happened?*			

Andreas could see that he knew what he meant but the reader (me!) might get confused. I left him with the whiteboard to turn his ideas into complete thoughts/sentences. Briefly putting their writing on a whiteboard makes it visible and easy for students to work with.

Conferencing with a sticky note as a scaffold

CONFERENCING WITH STICKY NOTES

Another way to conference to build sentences is by using a sticky note as a planning tool. I do this with mini-lessons but also with individual first graders during a conference. For example, Lyric wanted to write about her big sister Katherine but was stuck after writing, "I like my sister." As I asked questions, I took notes on sticky notes that could be used in writing. We used my whiteboard to practice writing each note as a complete sentence. I also showed Lyric how to check off each note as she writes a sentence.

CONFERENCING USING DIALOGUE

Sometimes we are humming along in Writing Workshop, but every once in a while it seems we are in the doldrums. Learning to write dialogue certainly spices up first grade writing. I came to this realization many years ago when conferencing with Elisha. She had a pig and horse talking in her farm story! I thought this was so interesting and so successful, I wanted to work on it in Writing Workshop. I asked Elisha to share as a mini-lesson the next day and wondered if the class would notice. I told them to listen for something different. "The animals are talking!" They got it, and we were off and running. Sure, writing dialogue can be tricky, especially with young writers, but it is worth the effort. Here are some steps I take:

Foundational Mini-Lesson: Dialogue in Literature

Using a variety of books as models, we look at dialogue. Sometimes people are talking, and sometimes the animals talk, like in Elisha's story.

Who said it?
- I send a student out of the room and then ask the rest of the class a simple question like, "What do you like for lunch?" I write a few of their responses down without the word "said" or the name of the speaker. The student returns and tries to guess who said what is written down. This activity makes the point that only people who heard the words would know.

- I add the word "said" to each line of print and the name of the speaker.

Key point: We use words like "said" and add names so the reader knows who is talking.

Say It, Write It: Using chart paper or a projector, we practice having two people talk and writing the conversation down. I use two different color pens so the speakers are easy to tell apart. Note: I am not going for punctuating dialogue yet, just getting the feel of a written conversation.

Key point: Conversations (things we say) can be written as dialogue.

Dialogue produces an award-winning writer!

One student, Stephen, shared a story he started in Author's Chair. I conferenced with him so he could practice the dialogue he wanted to use in his story. His two main characters were our beloved class pet, Nibbles the rat, and our boring class pet, the hermit crab. (My class has had more than one "Nibbles" over the years, but that was our only hermit crab; we never even named it because it did nothing!) Stephen brought them to life with dialogue and a Hawaiian adventure. This multi-page book was published in our classroom, and I entered it in the county Young Writer's Contest.

The Hermit Crab helped Nibbles get out of his cage. As they left Nibbles said, "Oops, I almost forgot the rope."

Page 3.

"Oh, where should we go?" asked the Hermit Crab. "We have a week off." said Nibbles, "How about a cheese store?" "NO." said the Hermit Crab, "How about Hawaii?"

Page 4.

Stephen tries dialogue in a story featuring Nibbles, our pet rat.

My favorite page is when Nibbles and the Hermit Crab were surfing and fell off their boards. They were saved by a giant crab that picked them up in enormous pinchers. The little Hermit Crab looks up and says, "Yo, cuz!" Yes, Stephen won the writing contest all those years ago.

But Stephen wasn't done yet. His mother contacted me in 2009 to say that he had published his first article just out of college—in *The Wall Street Journal*! You never know where engaging dialogue will take a story or a student!

Troubleshooting Tips

PROBLEM: The writing is flat and without details.

The Helping Hand and "5 W's" were taught thoroughly months ago, but in March I realize my students are clearly not asking themselves these questions about their own writing. It is time to revisit how to add details and make their stories more complete by asking *Who? What? Where? When?* and *Why?*

SOLUTION: Mini-Lesson, Focused Writing, Conferencing, Sharing

Mini-Lesson

1. Putting up my left hand, pinkie up/thumb down, I touch each finger starting with my pinkie and say, "Remember this: *Who, what, where, when, why?*"

2. "Do it with me." (with pinkie up)
   All repeat and touch their fingers, too.

3. Individual students open their journals and find yesterday's writing.
   I have them reread their writing. (This puts the story in their minds quickly.)
   Then I say, "Now read it again thinking about whether you know...

   Who or *what* is in the story?

   What happened?

   Where it happened?

   When it happened?

   Why it happened?"

4. Partners share stories and ask the questions on their fingers.
   Review who starts first and how to listen for the 5 W's using the Helping Hand.
   Teacher practices with one set of partners to model for all.
   Partners read to each other and ask questions.

Focused Writing

5. Class writes now, adding details to yesterday's writing, which they have just shared with a partner.

Conferencing

6. The teacher conferences with students, focusing on using their hand to ask the 5 W's.
   Conference first with the struggling writers or ELLs who might need extra support.

Sharing

7. Partners share again and count the details that have been added.

PROBLEM: No capitals and periods.

We have worked on capitals and periods for months, but it is still not sinking in for some students. Early in the year, most first graders do not use capitals and periods because the concept of a sentence is foreign. Oral language blends words together, often without breaks for a beginning and ending. Periods are a convention of writing that must be modeled, practiced, and encouraged all year. Knowing when a sentence starts dictates a capital, and knowing when it ends dictates a period.

SOLUTION: Find a more concrete way to teach the start of a sentence (capital letter) and the end (period).

It's time to get moving and tap into the auditory and kinesthetic learning modalities.

How:

1. Form a circle with the class.

2. Instead of sitting down, we crouch down low so that it is easy to pop up for a capital.

3. Teacher models a sentence that the class repeats. Teacher repeats the sentence, and pops up then down for the capital letter on the first word. On the last word, the teacher punches her clenched hand straight out to simulate putting a period at the end.

4. Various students give us a sentence that the group repeats and then acts out:
Pop up and down for the capital on the first word.
Punch out hand to simulate the period.

5. Repeat as time allows. Students will all want a turn, so this can take several sessions.

No periods

> **Tip**
>
> Have students immediately write their sentences down, starting with a capital and ending with a period.

Crouched down, ready to start a sentence

PROBLEM: Some students can't hold their sentence in memory.

The composing process can be difficult for first graders who have trouble holding the sentence they want to write in their mind. They can tell me their sentence but lose it sometimes when the sound-by-sound, letter-by-letter, word-by-word process becomes their whole focus.

SOLUTION: Create visual markers to stimulate memory.

One year, I had four students who kept losing track of what they were writing. I decided they needed a visual marker for each word.

How:

Small-Group Conference: Call students who needed scaffolding to the rug or other learning area. I model this process to remember each word:

1. I tell something (a complete sentence with a *Who* and *What happened.*) "My son Kevin plays football."

2. Students repeat my sentence slowly with me, and we touch a finger for each word. (Left palm up, start with thumb and go left to right.) Note: Most first graders only need to put the words on their fingers to remember the sentence.

3. Using the whiteboard, I draw a line for each word as we say the sentence again.

4. We count the lines and discover how many words I have to write (five).

5. With students' help, I write a word on each line.

6. Together, we reread my sentence while I point under each word written on a line. (Individual Conferences: I conference that day with the students who are in my small group.)

7. We repeat the process but use their sentences. I help them repeat the words and draw a line (in their journal) for each word.

8. I support writing each word on a line for the first sentence. Then, students generate a second sentence and draw lines for each word.

9. Students reread the sentence while pointing to the words on the lines. At this point I leave them to work independently.

Matthew will repeat his sentence and draw a line for each word.

This process of building sentence memory takes time. The line for each word is a visual scaffold that some students need. Saying it out loud as they point is a scaffold to hold it in auditory memory. One student, Matthew, used it for three weeks and then was able to remember what he was writing just by putting the words on his fingers.

Next Steps

I have given you many choices for getting help, procedures, assessment, mini-lessons, and conferences to keep your Writing Workshop going throughout first grade. Now, let's look at Revision, Editing, and Publishing with emergent writers. Chapter 4 will give you more choices for your own classroom and unique circumstances.

Writing Workshop: The Publication Process

Revising

Revision with first graders? Not easy—because typically once a six-year-old (and even some adults!) have written something, they consider it done (as in, set in cement!). So, don't wait 'til the last minute! At the Dublin conference in 1990, Donald Graves told us that the best revision comes early in a draft when there is a faint hint of "I might make this better." The majority of revision comes from the teacher in first grade. After all, do you know any young writers who ponder on their own "How can I make this piece better?"

Whole-Class Mini-Lessons for Strong Verbs, Amped-Up Adjectives, and Showing vs. Telling

Verbs, whether they carry action or feelings, don't usually carry much excitement in first grade writing. After the first couple of months, I want to build vocabulary and variety. This supports the Common Core State Standards in Vocabulary Acquisition: Distinguish shades of meaning among verbs differing in manner (e.g., *look, peek, glance, stare, glare, scowl*) and adjectives differing in intensity (e.g., *large, gigantic*) by defining or choosing them or by acting out the meanings [CSS.ELA-Literacy.L.1.5d].

VERB ACTION: Basics—and Beyond

I did a Web search for the most common verbs and then started an interactive word chart that we will work with on and off for months. A pocket chart is handy for this so the word cards can be moved around as new relationships are discovered. As a class, we discuss and act out the various nuances of some of the most common action verbs:

walk	run	skip	hop	jump	kick	
say	answer	tell	suggest	ask	listen	argue
start	begin	continue	stop			

The result of working with these verbs is that the students will try to include more variety in their writing. I tell them to avoid "The Yawn"—verbs that put the reader to sleep. They "get" that *saying something* is different from *arguing* when you say it. I have seen students like Marina move from repetitive phrases to interesting and meaningful sentences by adding varied and precise verbs.

We know that first graders stick to "safe" words because their vocabulary is limited OR they seem to use a word over and over because they know how to spell it. The words they use over and over are flat out boring (*nice, mad, glad, sad*). Word choice in first grade improves over time as we build vocabulary in specific mini-lessons that will

> my famly keep memrres
> inare harte. We rmebr
> inafunny way. I like
> that very much.
> I rmdr thim in a
> speshol way.

Marina's later writing uses a variety of verbs.

lead to revision. We also meet Common Core State Standards for First Grade Vocabulary Acquisition, when children use "adjectives differing in intensity (e.g., *large, gigantic*) by defining or choosing them or by acting out the meanings."

In depth vocabulary instruction impacts writing as well as reading comprehension. It is vital for all learners in all grades, but especially for our ELLs. Our emergent writers can get dependent on words like *nice, mad,* and *big.* Why not *friendly, furious,* and *humongous?*

SYNONYM STRETCH

A mini-lesson to build vocabulary by stretching a word's meaning with synonyms can be done anytime—and multiple times—throughout the year. For example, when we started a Science unit on dinosaurs, we did a brainstorming session on words to describe their size.

Synonyms can be posted for reference on a bulletin board that is built over time.

Synonym Stretch

Some words can also be added to your Word Wall. Think of words with many shades of meaning to brainstorm together. Below are some possibilities, but don't skip the student input; active involvement engages students and reinforces the learning. Dr. Isabel Beck's research in *Bringing Words to Life: Robust Vocabulary Instruction,* reminds us that long-term growth is possible—if we act out, demonstrate, and give multiple memorable concrete examples wherever possible.

A SAMPLE SYNONYM STRETCH

ask: question, inquire, quiz, interview, beg

baby: newborn, infant, toddler, tot

bad: naughty, evil, wicked, mischievous, miserable, lousy, awful, disgusting, wrong

big: large, giant, stout, stocky, huge, enormous, gigantic, humongous, colossal, massive

blue: navy, azure, turquoise, teal, royal blue, powder blue, baby blue, sky blue (Repeat with other colors periodically.)

bug: annoy, bother, tease, pester, irritate, disturb

cold: cool, chilly, icy, frosty, freezing, frigid, arctic

cry: whine, moan, groan, weep, sob, wail, bawl, whimper

dig: shovel, scoop, burrow, tunnel, plow, hoe

eat: devour, dine, feast, feed, gulp, gobble, wolf, gorge

funny: amusing, humorous, hilarious, witty

good: fine, excellent, outstanding, splendid, fair, great, kind

happy: glad, cheerful, joyful, jolly, delighted, ecstatic, pleased

jump: leap, spring, bound, hop, skip, pounce, hurdle

lake: pond, pool, lagoon, reservoir

mad: angry, furious, upset, annoyed, irate, cross

nice: good, great, delightful, polite, friendly, kind, fantastic

pretty: lovely, beautiful, gorgeous, stunning, dazzling

run: jog, trot, dash, bolt, dart, race, hurry

sad: unhappy, miserable, gloomy, moody, glum, depressed

talk: chat, tell, discuss, babble, gossip, blather

walk: stroll, march, hike, stride, plod, wander

yummy: tasty, delectable, savory, flavorful, delicious, scrumptious

A great source for more: *Scholastic Student Thesaurus,* 2007

SHOWING, NOT TELLING

"Show, Don't Tell" is a technique developed by Rebekah Caplan (*Writers in Training,* 1984) to help students write in a way that creates a picture in the reader's mind. The goal is to get away from just telling (*I have a messy room*) to showing what we would see, hear, smell, touch etc. in a messy room (*Clothes were strewn about the room. In fact, it was impossible to step anywhere without tripping over a skirt, a shirt, or a pair of dirty socks.*). Our work with adding details using the senses was foundational for this next step of showing as opposed to telling.

Modeled and shared writing work with mini-lessons on "showing" for just about every topic, including:

"The dinosaur was scary."

"Our teacher was mad."

"The kitten was in trouble."

"The fire drill went badly."

I model revision of these simple sentences (to "show"), and it leads to better writing overall. Of course, this takes time with first graders. For a mini-lesson on Show, Don't Tell, I used the boring sentence "The dinosaur was scary." I let the kids know that they don't have to believe what I said about the dinosaur in my story...they had to ask me questions to make me prove it. The hands went up:

Nick: "What did the dinosaur *do* that was scary?" I wrote: "The dinosaur pulled trees out of the ground as it came after me"

Aliyah: "Did he *look* scary?" I added: "It chomped its huge teeth that looked like big knives."

Ryan: "What did you do when it was chasing you?" I wrote: "I tore through the bushes as fast as I could to get away from the nasty teeth."

Jayly: "Why was the dinosaur chasing you?" I wrote: "I now was sorry I had looked into the nest of dinosaur eggs."

I paused and said: "Tell your partner what you hear and see now in my dinosaur story." We shared what our partners had told them and heard:

"I could see Mrs. Lynch running like crazy"

"I heard the dinosaur making huge booming noise with its feet."

"I heard Mrs. Lynch screaming."

"I saw trees flying all around the dinosaur."

We had a vote and they decided showing made better pictures in our heads. Next, we retitled my story using Synonym Stretch. What are other words than scary would better describe meeting this dinosaur?

scary   mean   angry   terrifying   frightening

I acted out each dramatically so my ELLs could catch the nuances of each choice. The class voted that the new idea to prove was "The dinosaur was terrifying." Then we looked at the sentences I had written to see if I had "proved it" by showing without just "telling."

New Title: "Dinosaur Terror"

The dinosaur pulled trees out of the ground as it came after me. It chomped its huge teeth that looked like big knives. I tore through the bushes as fast as I could to get away from the nasty teeth. I now was sorry I had looked into the nest of dinosaur eggs.

My experiences with six-year-old writers seems to affirm the need for massive modeling of stronger verbs and adjectives. Some will take it on in their own writing, and for others it is a foundation for writing in later grades.

Revision With the Teacher

For first graders, revision happens every day and does not often lead to publication. The craft of writing includes making it better. "Better" in a first grader's world starts with adding to a text that is incomplete. More intricate revision happens in the later grades, but we can make first graders accountable for: *clarity, details, extending,* and *expanding their writing.* The second day of school, I modeled adding to an incomplete story; revision started then and there. I model revision in mini-lessons and coach for it in individual conferences throughout the year.

Conferencing with Landon for revision

REVISION: ONE-TO-ONE CONFERENCE

Use the Helping Hand to Tell: Who? What? Where? When? Why?
The questioning we looked at for conferences in Chapters 2 and 3 often leads to additions and changes.

I don't understand… Tell me more about… What happened next?
Can you describe what that looks like?

Landon read his story about his dog Holly to me. I told him I didn't understand this sentence:

"Every time she sees something she does not want she still takes it."

Landon quickly explained that his dog will eat food even if it is not her favorite. I said that I was confused because when I first read it, I was worried that his dog was stealing things! So together we revised for meaning (we informed readers that the "what" is something to eat) by crossing out a couple of words and replacing them with new ones:

"Every time she sees something she does not [want], she still [takes] it."
                                       like to eat   eats

Revision With Peers and Buddies

Peer revision? I'm sure you're thinking, "Isn't that for older writers?" Yes, in its most advanced form. But we can model and practice peer revision during Author's Chair, with buddies, in small groups, and with partners.

Win I caem to this
Schoel I like it at first

Enasia's writing before she shared it with peers during Author's Chair

When I came to this
school I liked it at first.

Win I caem to this
Schoel I like it at first
I wus shyd now I am not
shyd I got fiends and a now
techer and now fiends.

Enasia's revision after peer feedback during Author's Chair

When I came to this
school I liked it at first.
I was shy. Now I am not
shy. I got friends and a new
teacher and new friends.

REVISING AFTER AUTHOR'S CHAIR

Sharing a work in progress in Author's Chair is fundamental to peer revision. After hearing a piece, the hands shoot up with compliments and questions (especially the "5 Ws," so keep the Helping Hand chart posted nearby). At the start of the year, students used to say things like, "I like your story" and "Your pictures are nice." No opportunity for the writer to improve there! After our mini-lessons on questioning, adding details, and words choice, the feedback is much more productive. I will still have to model how to think about what might be missing in the author's story: *Do we know who or what it is about? What is happening or what are we learning? Where does it take place? When does it happen? Why is that happening or why did you do that?* Again, the Helping Hand chart is crucial. And, of course, we will end up asking the question word not on the hand: "how." *How did that happen? How did that turn out? How did you feel?*, etc. Author's Chair becomes a powerful tool for peer revision when we conclude by asking the writer, "What might you add to or change in your writing?" For example, Enasia decided to add *why* she wasn't shy at her new school anymore as a result of the questions her peers had asked.

BUDDY HELP

When the upper-grade buddies first start helping me, I have them listen in as I conference with a student. It is on-the-job training. I explain as I go that I am looking to clarify, extend, or expand on the writing. Buddies have a copy of the "Content Conference Guide" (Reproducible 9) in hand when they observe my conferences, and when they are working with a student. Soon buddies (and volunteer parents) are able to make an important contribution to revising writing. Sometimes buddies/parent volunteers worry that they won't ask the "right" question. I reassure them that when the writing is not clear, the questions come naturally. One day, Lucas was conferencing with Jonathon and included Gabby in the feedback.

6th-Grade Buddy Lucas gives feedback for revision to Jonathon and gets Gabby involved.

Here is what Jonathon wrote and read to Lucas and Gabby:

I went to take my dog on a walk. I went to take my dog to the store.
She dropped her ice cream cone. I got another ice cream cone.
I got her another ice cream cone.

What do you think Lucas and Gabby asked Jonathon in order to clarify his story about his dog? They asked exactly what I would have asked: "How did your dog drop an ice cream cone?" Jonathon explained that he was holding the cone and his dog knocked it accidentally to the ground with a big lick. Aha! One of the key pieces to revision is to realize that first graders know exactly what they mean—but it is all in their head! What they need to learn is the idea of audience and how to get it all down on paper for that audience to read and understand. I am always happy to have volunteers (students and parents) to help with Writing Workshop. It is essential to have this extra set of ears to listen and give feedback because there is only one of me!

READ-AROUND IN A SMALL GROUP

To maximize the use of my time, I meet with a group of three or four students who give each other feedback on a draft. They each get a turn to read their draft and answer questions from the group. Each time I do this with a new group, there are procedures to model and practice:

ACTIVE LISTENING
• sit quietly
• hands folded
• lean forward
• look at the writer
• think of questions

Active Listening: I have fun modeling what NOT to do. While one member in the group reads his or her piece, I rock back and forth in my chair, talk to my neighbor, drum my pencil on the table, play with my shoe, etc. You get the idea. Then we talk about what was wrong with my behavior. We make a list for Active Listening and practice it that day:

GIVING FEEDBACK	
"I don't understand…"	(CLARIFY)
"Tell me more about…"	(EXPAND)
"What do you plan to do next?"	(EXTEND)

Giving Feedback: Next we talk about how we can help each other with questions and suggestions to clarify, extend, and expand the writing. We use the Helping Hand chart for questions, and I make a simple chart featuring typical "teacher feedback" that they have heard in my conferences.

PARTNER REVISION WITH CONTENT

Later in first grade, depending on the class *this* year, I will do some partner feedback for revision. Students have had many experiences doing this with classmates in Author's Chair, with Buddies or Parents, or in small groups doing a read-around.

For a "partner revision" mini-lesson, I model the following. (Initially I partner with a student for the modeling; then I observe two students doing partner feedback.)

1. Listen to a partner:
   Ask your partner the basic "teacher feedback" questions and give feedback. Switch roles and get feedback.

2. Partners practice with observing and listening in.
   I remind students about active listening behavior, Helping Hand questions, and "teacher style" feedback as necessary.)

PARTNER REVISION WITH WORD CHOICE

Banishing Boredom

We have done many mini-lessons with me taking the lead on expanding on verbs and stretching synonyms. It is time for partners to give it a go. . . and for me to move about the room giving support.

Modeling Partner Revision Work With One Student

1. With the rest of the class close by, I model with Preston as we circle the verbs in his journal writing. I think out loud: "We are looking for action and feeling words to circle and see if we can improve on them."

2. We read the first sentence, *I went to my aunts's house*, and I ask Preston, "Where is the action that shows what *I* did?" He circles *went*. "*Went* is an action that shows that you moved. But how exactly did you *get* to your aunts's house? Did you fly in a plane, ride on a bus, take a train?" Preston piped up, "I walked to her house." "Does that show your readers better how you got there?" The class agrees that *walked* makes his story better.

Modeling partner work with Preston

3. We did the same process with *I like my aunt's house*, and he agreed that his aunt's house was his favorite place to visit, so he changed it to: *I love my aunt's house.*

Partner Practice

Turning six-year-olds loose to do this takes some faith in the process. We have done partner work all year, so that procedure is in place. I think of my English Language Learners and others needing help and match them with appropriate partners. I do this towards the end of the school year and use it to challenge my advanced writers. For the others, I roam quickly to get them started and praise any attempts by announcing verbs that have been circled. We gather back on the rug after about 10 minutes and quickly call on partners to share their verbs while I chart them and the revisions.

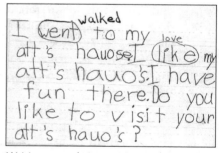

Writing sample improving verbs

Self-Revision in First Grade

When I first started Writing Workshop all those years ago, I had the mistaken notion that revision and editing were primarily part of the publication process. I was right that I would encourage some revision and do the final edit to prepare a book to publish. But it soon dawned on me that improving the craft of writing and learning accurate spelling, capitals, and punctuation is a daily job. I decided that first graders can take on some responsibility early on in the school year. To keep it simple, I follow this plan after modeling each procedure:

Partners revising

3 Minutes Before Stopping = Self-Revision and Self-Editing

Revising Your Work

When: 3 Minutes Before Stopping

How:

1. Stop Signal

   We practice the day before what is expected when I give the signal. (I use the chimes.) They can finish the word they are writing, and then the pencil goes down and the hands go up.

2. Softly reread every word.

   Each student whisper reads what he or she wrote that day. If some students have trouble concentrating, they can use a reading phone.

What:

Students practice over many days, asking themselves three questions:

Does it make sense?   (meaning)
Does it sound right?   (structure of English grammar)
Does it look right?   (spelling/handwriting/neatness)

Then…No erasing!

Students need to know that we need to see their "first tries" at revision so we can see how much progress they are making and show their parents. One red line through the word is all that is needed. They learn to write a better spelling above the crossed out word. They learn to use a caret to add words they left out. They need help all year with end punctuation and capitals, so they should mark their revisions in red pencil so we can see where they still need support. To help with this "3-Minute Revise and Edit," I also give students a copy of the "I Edit My Writing" checklist to keep in their folder (Reproducible 17).

Red pencil edits only:

- Add words left out.
- Cross out extra words.
- Use end punctuation (. ? !).
- Capitalize the first word in a sentence; names; and *I*.
- Circle shaky spellings.
- Fix above the word. (Fix spelling and word choice by writing above a crossed out word. Use word lists and word wall as resources.)

Over time, a quick daily revision pays off and makes first graders accountable for trying to make that day's writing better. It establishes a work ethic that will lay the foundation for self-revision and self-editing as they grow as writers over the next few years of elementary school.

Self-revision and editing using a "reading phone"

To make "reading phones," take a ten foot section of 1" PVC pipe (available at home improvement stores) cut into 3" segments. Attach a 1" elbow piece to each end. These "phones" are also useful to keep first grade voices low when kids are reading independently. This quiet reading goes straight to their own ear and helps them "hear" when something is not right. When *they* hear it out loud, they often can self-correct. Just three minutes a day can provide a format for independent revision.

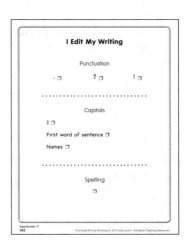

why I work up ^is because

Alana uses a caret to add the word "is" when her reading doesn't make sense.

Editing

Materials:

There are a variety of materials that can be used for editing. They can be placed in an Editing Center or given to each student.

"I Edit My Writing" Checklist (Reproducible 17)

Red pencils (self edit/no erasing)

High-Frequency Word Lists (Reproducibles 2, 3, 4, 5)

ABC Chart (Reproducible 1)

Simple Dictionaries

Word Wall

Personal Word Wall (created with Reproducible 1)

"Skills _____ Can Do as a Writer" Chart (Reproducible 11)

Editing for Punctuation

I do a series of mini-lessons over time to build in review and next steps that are slightly more challenging.

Punctuation Takes a Vacation by Robin Pulver is a delightful book to use for a mini-lesson. It captures the attention of first graders when the class is stranded because the punctuation went to "Take-a-Break Lake." Mr. Wright's class writes a jumbled message using punctuation from the class next door where it had been "running wild." For example:

Please come! back We need you? We, miss, you, too.
Life at? school is! "difficult" without, you?

As a whole-class activity, I read aloud the book, and we stop and discuss what is wrong and how to fix it.

READING PUNCTUATION

Punctuation carries meaning. To make this point, I introduce "punctuation cards," which we use to practice punctuation over time—this isn't a one-time lesson! (To make cards for your students, use standard index cards or copy punctuation marks onto cardstock.)

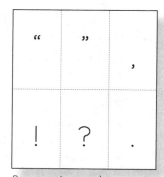

Punctuation cards

1. Learn about punctuation marks.
How:

I make a copies on cardstock, and give first graders kid-friendly (see chart on page 109 for examples) definitions and uses for a period, question mark, exclamation point, quotation marks, and the comma. Then students practice each form of punctuation.

Punctuation Marks	
.	The period is a stop sign at the end of a telling sentence. Our voice stays normal. Practice. (Have students practice making simple statements.)
?	The question mark comes at the end of an asking sentence. Our voice goes a little higher at the end of a question. Practice. (Have students practice asking questions out loud.)
!	The exclamation point (or "excitement mark" as we sometimes call it) is at the end of a sentence that shows excitement, strong emotion, or strong commands. Our voice shows excitement and strong feelings. Practice. (Have students practice exclaiming or demanding things.)
" ... "	The quotation marks, or "talking marks" show the words someone says and dialogue. Our voice changes to sound like the person talking. Practice. (Have students practice reading aloud and changing their voices to sound like the character speaking.) Note: This may be a lesson for only those students who are ready. In first grade, I teach students to recognize "talk marks" when reading, but do not necessarily require them in student's own writing unless they are ready for it.
,	The comma shows where to slow down when reading or where lists of things are being separated. Our voice slows a little and then goes on. Practice. (Have students practice reading aloud sentences with commas.)

2. Model "Three Ways to End Three Sentences"
   How:
   Teacher models three kinds of end punctuation in a personal story, and students practice reading each example out loud.
   On another day, I quickly write three sentences that need end punctuation: a period, a question mark, and exclamation mark. The class practices reading my story and changing their voices. Together we decide which sentences are: telling, asking, exclaiming.

3. Model "Three Ways to End One Sentence"
   Materials:
   End Punctuation Cards (. ? !)
   Pocket Chart
   Three Sentence Strips to write the same sentence: *The principal is here.*
   How:
   Review the end punctuation cards: their purpose and how our voices change with each one.

Three sentences to show three types of end punctuation

Put up the same sentence (three times) about the principal with no end punctuation. Mix up the Punctuation Cards, pull one out dramatically, and place it at end of first strip.

Read with great drama, for example: The principal is here? (a surprised questioning tone)

Repeat with the other cards and read each with voice changes:

The principal is here! (an excited tone)

The principal is here. (a neutral tone)

As an extension of this activity, read a sentence aloud, and have students choose which punctuation mark belongs at the end. Make photocopies of end punctuation cards for each student. After you say a sentence (statement, question, or exclamation) aloud, children should hold up the appropriate end punctuation card.

Don't be surprised if your first graders over-use punctuation for a time as they flex their dramatic muscle. Remember, the whole point of punctuation is to help the writing make sense and carry meaning to the audience.

ey. One day a **Gragin atack** !|||!||!|| It has'et happend sience 1650 and it was 1980.

It is common to see punctuation used with gusto when first graders start using it.

Student samples to practice reading sentences

Using student work for mini-lessons always brings the strategy up close and personal for first grade writers. Sarah offers to let us read her sentences with voice changes for punctuation. After we read each sentence as punctuated, the class discusses the type of sentence. Getting familiar with telling, asking, and exclamations takes time with emergent writers.

When punctuation is not used properly, another mini-lesson to practice how to read and place a period, question mark, and exclamation point is in order. Brian let us use his "Bats in America" story to practice. He decided when we read them as is, that the last line (*But most of all I love bats*) needed an "exclamation" mark. We also discussed the "talking mark" (quotation mark) that was randomly used.

Sarah models punctuation in front of the class. Students repeat each sentence and check punctuation for: Telling, Asking, Exclaiming.

My fish is cute. They are
fun. They make me laugh.
I fed them a lot of times.
Do you like fish?

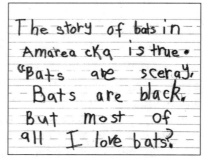

Bryan lets us use his bats story to practice reading punctuation.

The story of bats in
America is true.
"Bats are scary.
Bats are black.
But most of
all I love bats?

Conference Connections

The mini-lessons on punctuation will make the usual connections for conferencing and working with student writing. The teacher, student helpers, and parent volunteers will all have copies of the Punctuation Cards to use when with working with students. The visual aids make the mini-lessons more concrete when connecting to student writing.

Editing for Spelling

SELF-EDITING FOR SPELLING IN MINI-LESSONS

Emma and other brave first graders will edit for spelling on the projector for all to see. Students know that Emma will circle words that look funny to her.

I am a princess
and I have a cat.
Then my friend Gabby
came. She was
a princess too. Her name was Gabby.

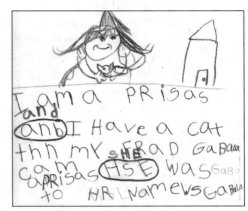

Emma edits for spelling in front of the class

In this mini-lesson, the goal is to illustrate self-editing, not to edit every word she missed.

If I take over, it diminishes the student effort. In first grade, a self-edit is a success if students can find some words to circle. It becomes a triumph when these words are self-corrected using recall, a word wall, or other resources in the classroom.

TEACHER EDITS DURING A STUDENT CONFERENCE

I saw this rabbit it was
white and pretty and it had
blue eyes and I took it home
it was talking on the way home.

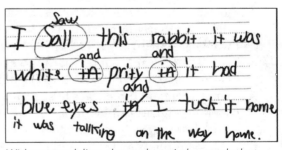

With my modeling, the student circles words that don't look like they are spelled right.

With my encouragement, the student circles words that don't look like they are spelled right. This is basic spelling editing—looking for words that "look funny." When students have had a lot of experience reading words and spelling them from the word wall, they can usually spot those that don't match the spelling in their visual memory. This is a skill we all use for the rest of our lives. I often write both spellings of a word I am not sure of (*beleive* or *believe*) to see which one "looks right."

EDITING WITH A PERSONAL WORD WALL

I create personal word walls on cardstock. Some first graders are ready for more advanced high-frequency words before they are put on the class Word Wall. Some need review words or family names close at hand. Others need the words on the Word Wall closer visually—they can't visually track from the wall to their paper. A personal word wall does all this and slips into the left pocket of their writing folders. The teacher or a class helper usually adds any needed words neatly to the form.

STUDENT EDITS

There are many resources that have been modeled and practiced over the first five months of the school year. Students know to check spelling daily during the last three minutes before stopping when I give the signal. The "I Edit My Writing" checklist reminds them what to prepare for publication. First grade writing folders have high-frequency word lists at their finger tips. Students use the lists that meet their needs.

Landon edits "friend" with a high-frequency word list.

The classroom Word Wall also builds throughout the year and is always a source for editing.

"FIXING" SPELLING—FIRST GRADE STYLE

I have taught students to circle words that don't look right in red pencil, but can they fix them? In general, we all know that when six- and seven-year-olds correct their own spelling it can be sketchy at best. But, there are ways to get them involved and be responsible for the effort. Early mini-lessons on how to spell words give them a way to "have a go" at spelling words. Mid-year I will revisit "3 Ways to Spell a Word," but will use it for editing spelling. They know there are three ways to spell words (arm spelling, rubber band writing, and Word Wall/ word lists). Now, however, the mini-lessons will focus on using these methods to check the words circled in red.

Lexus uses the word wall as a resource.

1. Look at the Word Wall or Word List

   The students take out their writing journals and pick a rough draft they can use to circle words that might be misspelled. Using the projector, I have several students write the word they circled, and we project them for all to problem solve.

   Word Wall Search:
   > Look at first letter of the problem word.
   > Say the word to spell.
   > Find the letter box on the Word Wall. Do I see the word? (Practice searching as a group.)
   > *If I find the word, I write it over the circled word.*
   > *If I don't find the word on the Word Wall, I can use the. . .*

Word Lists Search:

> Use high-frequency word lists in writing folder.
> Say the word to spell.
> Find the letter box on the word list. Do I see the word? (Practice searching as a group.)
> *If I find the word, I write it over circled word.*
> *If I don't find the word on the Word Lists, I can. . .*
> (refer to 2 or 3 below)

2. Sound out a short word on my arm.

    The first graders know that they can spell a short word on their left arm. Together we practice some short words that I supply that are not on the Word Wall or word lists:

    frog   snap   jump

    How:

    Look at the circled word and say it out loud (for example, "fg").

    Touch right hand to the top of left shoulder.

    Say the sounds slowly and tap down the arm for each sound. (/f/ /r/ /o/ /g/)

    What letters could be added or changed? (We add letters in the middle of "frog": *r* and *o*)

    Edit spelling: Write "frog" over the circled spelling "fg."

3. Spell longer words by stretching out the sounds (rubber-band writing).

    Tapping sounds from the top to the bottom of the arm works best on short words. For longer words, we review "rubber-band writing" and use it for editing a circled word. The practice word might be something like "dnr" for "dinosaur."

    How:

    Look at the circled word ("dnr") and say it out loud, "dinosaur."

    Pretend to stretch word like a rubber band:

    > Put fingertips on both hands together.
    > Pull the fingers apart slowly.
    > Stretch and say the sounds while looking at the word to edit.

    What letters could be added or changed? (students heard /i/ /o/ /s/)

    Edit spelling over the circled word: write *dinosr* above *dnr.*

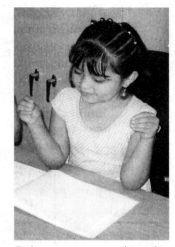

Dulce practices stretching the sounds in "dinosaur."

Using arm spelling and rubber-band writing to spell a word can improve first graders phonetic spelling. The editing over the circled word may not necessarily be the exact spelling, but it is usually a good approximation that gets closer over time. Paying attention to more and more of the sounds and letters in a word is a step in the right direction.

Publishing & Presenting

Final Edit for Publication

In the five-stage writing process, publishing is the last piece. When I first started doing Writing Workshop, I thought it was the most important part. As you can imagine, I drove myself crazy. I was spending so much time on publishing that the first graders weren't

Class volunteer Mrs. Sockwell helps with the final edit.

Marina and Sebastian are working quietly at the table dedicated to the Publishing Center.

doing the writing needed for growth over time. Donald Graves set me straight when he told us at the Dublin conference that the rule of thumb was to publish every fourth or fifth piece. He said students need to have a body of work to choose something of value. The goal is not to grind it out and expect most everything to be published. Of course, he was talking to teachers from grades K-12. I have learned to come up with my own first grade rule of thumb: Publish occasionally, but keep my sanity in the process! The final edit for publication is done by me, but I get help to make it easier. A parent volunteer or intermediate-grade buddy can help do the first edit for spelling, capitals, and punctuation.

Writing daily in draft form is still the primary focus with first graders. With that said, let's look at options for publishing resources, procedures, formats, and audiences.

RESOURCES TO SUPPORT PUBLISHING

Dedicated Area for a Classroom Publishing Center
Set up a table that can be used for book making.

Materials in a Classroom Publishing Center
Tote or Basket to hold materials. (The basket can be stored on a shelf when not in use.)

Supplies
    glue sticks
    special pens, colored pencils, crayons
    temporary publishing folder for each student (to keep publishing materials in one place)
    stapler
    scissors

Covers (your choice of book size and paper):
    full size: cardstock (8.5" x 11")
                construction paper (9" x 12")
    half size: cardstock (4.5" x 5.5")
                construction paper (4" x 6")

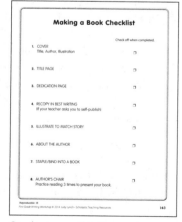

Students use this form when they are getting a book ready for publication.

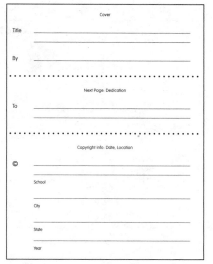

Title/About the Author form

Cover/Dedication/Copyright form

Forms

The forms on pages 115 and 116 are examples of the kinds of "how-to" guides and letters I send home to parents who are typing books for us. We all have our own teaching style and personality, so use these as models for creating your own instructions and letters for parents. The templates you create should give the parent "publishers" guidelines on how to type the Title/Copyright/Dedication pages, About the Author page, and interior pages. Generally, when sending home material, students will copy their edited drafts onto your templates *in their best handwriting.* (If their writing is too difficult to copy, you or a buddy can transfer student writing onto forms.)

In-school forms (students, teachers, or buddies fill in at school):
Title/About the Author form; Cover/Dedication/Copyright form; interior book pages (with lines and page-number indicator)

Send-home forms:
Parent-Publisher Letter; book forms prepared in school by students; Parent-Publisher Guidelines (Text Layout, Font, Margins and Printing Guides form; Publishing Sample—Cover/Dedication/Copyright form)

Other possible materials: copies of student photos for the About the Author page

My students copy their edited pages onto forms like these. This shows parents typing at home the format and order of the book pages.

Finally, once a student's book is complete (typed, illustrated, and "published"), I send it home to the family along with a Congratulations letter. I always ask families to return the book to school with their child, so we can keep it in our classroom library to be enjoyed by the other students. At the end of the year, students' books will be sent home for families to keep and treasure.

Parent-Publisher Letter (Sample 1)

Dear First Grade Parent-Publishers,

Thank you for offering to type our books at home and be part of our "Publishing Team." I will send the materials home with your first grader in a large manila envelope labeled "Class Stories for Publication." Please return the finished pages in the envelope as soon as possible. Inside you will find paper clipped:

1. Sample pages that show the layout for

Cover/ Title Page

Dedication/Copyright Information

Page layout for student writing

About the Author

Information on margins, font and printing

2. A typed book as a finished example of margins and layout.

3. One or more stories to be typed

Pages may be handwritten by me or a volunteer with the Cover, Title Page, Dedication, About the Author and page layouts indicated.

OR… It may be a copy from the student's writing journal that has been edited for final publication.

If you have any questions, please call me anytime or contact me if you would like a quick training session!

Sincerely,

Parent-Publisher Letter

Parent-Publisher Guidelines (Sample 2)

Text Layout, Font, Margins and Printing Guides

Left Margin: 1"+ to allow for stapling the finished book

Leave the top 1/3 to 1/2 of the page for an illustration.

Font Size: Typically large and easy to read depending on how much text is on a page.

This sample is 18 Comic Sans with 24 pt leading.

Page Number

Typical Page Layout for Last Page

We try to do an About the Author page at the end of every book. Please leave the top area for a photograph or self drawn picture of the author.

About the Author

Printing

Thank you for typing and printing these pages. Please paper clip the copied pages with the originals for each book. New first grade authors are eagerly awaiting their books to illustrate and share.

Parent-Publisher Guidelines

Parent-Publisher Guidelines (Sample 3)

Publishing Sample: Cover Page/Dedication/Copyright

Cover Page Layout

Font: Comic Sans is the easiest to read

Title

Author

My New Kitten

by
Joshua Hayes

Next page

Dedication

Copyright:
date
School's Name
City, State

Dedicated
to
My Mom and Dad

Copyright
October 14, 2013
Ridgepoint School
Sacramento,
California

Parent-Publisher Guidelines

Sample Congratulations Letter (Sample 4)

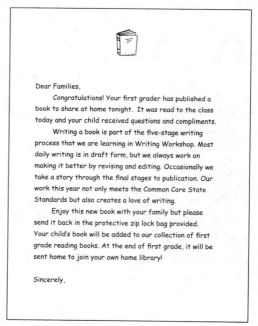

Dear Families,

Congratulations! Your first grader has published a book to share at home tonight. It was read to the class today and your child received questions and compliments.

Writing a book is part of the five-stage writing process that we are learning in Writing Workshop. Most daily writing is in draft form, but we always work on making it better by revising and editing. Occasionally we take a story through the final stages to publication. Our work this year not only meets the Common Core State Standards but also creates a love of writing.

Enjoy this new book with your family but please send it back in the protective zip lock bag provided. Your child's book will be added to our collection of first grade reading books. At the end of first grade, it will be sent home to join your own home library!

Sincerely,

Sample Congratulations Letter

Publishing Center at School Using Student Helpers or Parent Volunteers

We can also get help with publishing if parents are willing to type books at school. Some schools have parents who come in and prepare books for the school, for a grade level, or more than one classroom. I like to have the parents take a student or two with them to watch the process. This can be at the back of my classroom at a computer, or with other parents in a common center, or in a media center if your school has one. The Common Core State Standards support this: "With guidance and support from adults, use a variety of digital tools to produce and publish writing, including in collaboration with peers" (CCSS.ELA-Literacy.W.1.6).

I can use the same forms that show how to lay out the text for parents helping out from home. A quick training session can help parents at home or school understand this simple but important process.

Procedures for Publishing—Mini-Lessons

It is time to do more procedural mini-lessons when the first small group of authors starts publishing. I keep track of who is publishing by putting a "P" by their name on my clipboard on the first day they begin the process. First graders will catch the excitement and ask when they will have a turn to publish. I show my clipboard and remind them that they will each have a turn before anyone makes a second book. I will publish a variety of levels of writing to start the year. For instance, an emerging writer who has written three sentences about his cat can make a three-page book.

TEACHER MODELS THE PROCESS

In a mini-lesson, I will model the process with a student sample (Richard's). I will make it clear that Richard's finished book will have the spelling, capitals, and punctuation that is standard in published writing.

With the author, we decide where to layout the pages, usually when the topic or focus changes. I show several samples for publication, and the student and I collaborate on which they might choose.

Depending on a student's handwriting prowess: I can copy it into a book, the student can recopy it into a book, a 6th-grade buddy or parent volunteer can type it, or a copy can be sent home for a parent to type and print.

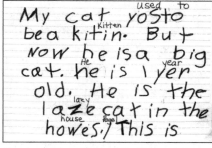

Final teacher edit modeled in a mini-lesson with Richard's cat story.

STUDENTS HELP WITH THE FINAL EDIT

Before publishing, Joseph does a final edit on the projector for all to see. As a class, we consider the capitals, spelling, and end punctuation using the "I Edit My Writing" Checklist.

Joseph offers to let the class assist in a final edit with his facts about tree frogs. He numbers the sentences because he has lots of telling sentences. With class support, he makes the final corrections so he can publish "The Frog." This entails more editing than a

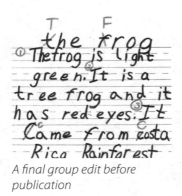

A final group edit before publication

regular mini-lesson but is an important example of students helping each other. They did ask me to get out the dictionary to spell "picture" because they knew something was not right with "picher."

ORGANIZATION: USING A TEMPORARY PUBLISHING FOLDER

Organizing all the pages and front and back covers for a book can be daunting for a first grader. I do a mini-lesson so the class gets to see the special "Publishing Folder" to help book makers organize their materials.

These are regular folders with pockets inside to hold all the paperwork and keep it clean and smooth. Students making a book keep their yellow folders in the tote while they are at the Publishing Center. I put their name on the outside with peel off Post-It® tape so the same folders can be reused all year. The boys model taking out one page at a time from the left pocket to illustrate. I show the class how to return a finished page carefully to the right pocket. The time taken in this mini-lesson pays off for all future authors. We put in too much effort to have published pages get smushed, crumpled, bent, or torn.

USING SPECIAL FORMS AND ART SUPPLIES

A mini-lesson to look at the publishing tote incudes what is inside, how to keep it organized, and the clean-up expectations.

Contents of a publishing tote

Contents of a publishing tote:

Yellow folders to organize materials for each author

Covers in cardstock

Templates for self-publishing a book: "About the Author"; Title/Dedication/Copyright page; special art supplies that are only used for book making

PROCEDURES FOR MAKING A BOOK

The "Making a Book Checklist" is an optional form for Writing Workshop. Some students would get totally confused by it, and others benefit from its step-by-step directions. Mini-lessons on each section are done when we first start publishing. This chart is in the tote. Once the book pages are neatly written or typed and illustrated, children (independently or with assistance) create a cover, a title page, a dedication page, complete an "About the Author," and then staple or bind the book together.

When students are able to take over part of the task, I teach them how to write a draft of their own "About the Author" page in their writing journal. I post a list of possible information to include:

Name
Age
Hometown
Favorite school subjects, writing topics, foods, games
Interesting facts

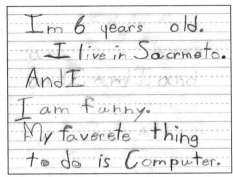

Alyssa's own "About the Author" before it is edited and typed on the computer.

What we will see and hear in the Publishing Center

In my first grade classroom, every literacy center has procedures to follow. At the beginning of the year, we brainstorm and chart what we will "see" and "hear" at that center. When it is time to start publishing in Writing Workshop, we make a similar chart for book-making. These charts put us all on the same page with the expectations for work and behavior. Periodically, the charts will be reviewed to make sure independent work is productive.

PROCEDURES FOR ILLUSTRATIONS

Illustrations are an important piece in bookmaking but they can pose problems. I need to model the procedure as to where to put the pictures or some students will color over the print on the page. Then I dig into *why* a picture is put on the page. Using picture books, we examine how the illustrations support the story or facts. On another day, my mini-lesson includes drawing a quick picture for my story about our dog jumping in our pool. Thinking out loud as I color, I put the key elements into the background. Because I had written about getting splashed, we talked about how to draw that. Soon, light blue water drops are all over me in the picture. When I am done, I ask for thumbs up or down to evaluate my picture matching my words.

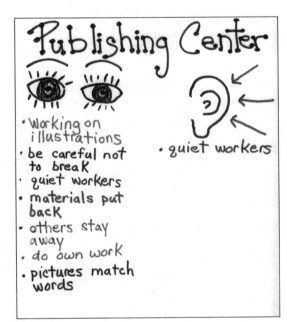

What we will "see" and "hear" at the Publishing Center

I model doing an illustration and get thumbs up that my illustration matches the words.

The next day, Gabby offers to let us look at her illustrations and evaluate the match to her text. She reads one page at a time, and then we look carefully at the picture. She colors a typical first grade illustration with no background on the white paper; we ask if there is a "snowstorm" since it is all white. Gabby gets some gentle suggestions to put the same details into her illustrations that she has into her words.

Does Gabby's picture match her words?

Format for Publication Options

The format for how to publish a book depends on what the student needs and what help is available.

TEACHER RECOPIES IN FRONT OF CHILD

For my most emergent writers, I can make a book right in front of them. I use their text and transfer it to my templates for book-making (cover, title, inside pages, etc.). I make small teaching points but don't overwhelm the author. After each page is copied by me, the student practices reading it, and we discuss the picture that would match their words. Then we put it in one of the yellow publishing folders and the book-making can begin.

Teacher recopies book pages in front of the student author. The author, Dulce, made her own cover for "Eggs."

STUDENT RECOPIES

Making their own books takes good handwriting and the ability to copy from their journal to the template pages. The goal is that the book is easily readable with uniform letter shapes and spaces. When I notice a students who can handle this, I walk them through the process but let them be independent. They copy from the rough draft in their journal that we edited together. After copying and making a book or two under my watchful eye, some first graders can do this on their own.

Janessa can't wait to read her new book to her big sister when she picks her up after school

Cover of Janessa's book

Inside page of Janessa's book

PARENTS TYPE BOOKS AT HOME

When I first started Writing Workshop with my class, I typed all the books myself. As you can imagine, that got old fast. I loved having parents help at school and realized that someone's mom or dad might be willing to type for us at home. As it turned out, it has often been a working parent who likes to stay connected to what is happening at school. There is great prestige for the first graders who take home the large manila envelopes and return with printed pages. Now, I recruit members of our "Publishing Team" using the parent letters in the fall (such as a Parent Volunteer form and a Writing Workshop letter). I always send home a Parent-Publisher Guidelines letter and sample book; reviewing margins, fonts, layout, and printing gives them confidence.

BUDDIES TYPE AT SCHOOL

How to set up computer for Buddy/First Grader use:

A great source of help in publishing are trained upper-grade students with good keyboarding skills. The first grade stories are edited beforehand and marked by pages. I place some templates for the computer with easy-to-follow directions in one file and a writing folder for each student on the desktop.

6th-grade buddy Lucas types Matthew's baseball book.

Student Folders on Computer Desktop
Each student has a folder for saving book pages before and after printing.

Book Templates
I instruct helpers to go to the "Template for Typing a New Book Folder" that I have created on the desktop. This folder has the Title Page and Page Layout templates. Prior to this, I have met with my volunteers after school to train them in using the templates and saving into student folders. It takes some practice to get into the rhythm of:

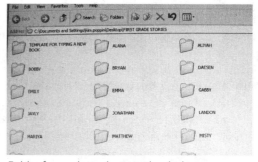

Folder for each student on the desktop

Type on template

Print

"Save As" into a student's folder

The Title Page template shows the layout for the title page and reminds the helper how to save the work with the student's name into their folder on the desktop. It is important that when helpers finish printing a page, they use the "Save As" feature to rename the page for the student.

The template for layout of text to allow for picture on top, page number, and instructions on how to save and label for student's folder on desktop.

The Page Layout template shows where to start typing (about 4 inches from the top) in order to allow room for the illustration on the top. It reminds helpers to put in the page number and to "Save As" by renaming the file and saving to the student's folder on the desktop.

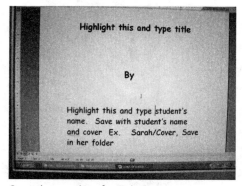

Sample template for Title Page

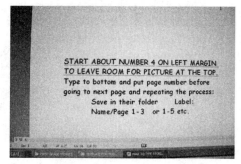

Page layout guidelines

AUDIENCE OPTIONS

Author's Chair
New first grade authors practice reading their new book to me, or to volunteers or classmates.

This front loads them for a successful fluent reading in Author's Chair. This is their first audience and they will get questions and compliments fitting a finished piece.

When the students have presented to the class in Author's Chair, the book goes home that night with the proud author (in a zip lock bag along with a letter to the family). I ask families to send the book back so we can make it part of our library of published books. Student books will go home at the end of the school year, however, so they can be part of treasured first grade memories.

Partners
Six- and seven-year-olds love to read each other's books. To make that successful, they ask the author to read the book to them first during "Drop Everything and Read." (This usually happens after lunch.) Hearing the book read by the author first is crucial because even if they've heard it once in Author's Chair doesn't mean they can read the other child's book independently.

Sharing in Author's Chair

Kindergarten

Eager audiences for first grade books are the Kindergarten children nearby. Periodically we write a letter to former teachers to see if it is "convenient" for a small group of the new authors to read their writing. When they do, the authors usually sit informally on the rug and read to small groups.

School Assembly

Ridgepoint School follows our long district tradition and has "Morning Sing" every Friday morning. It is a community event, and parents who have just brought their children to school often stay. We sing seasonal songs, give student awards, and celebrate new authors. The teachers can showcase an author on a rotating basis. I always call the parents when I can feature a first grader in this special forum. We have a stool for the student to sit on, and a teacher holds the microphone so everyone can hear.

Author's Tea

A simple get together that includes families is a popular way to feature authors. It can occur several times a year, if you have lots of help, or it may be a one-time spring event. The students write the invitations, and families can provide lemonade and cookies. Guests listen to their own first grader and then move around the room informally to hear other authors. A simple alternative is to feature the books at Open House in the spring.

Sharing with families at Author's Tea

Read to Class Next Door

Want to keep it really simple and have a quick audience? I have a deal with the teacher next door. We check in with each other when we have an authors "touring group" ready. We arrange to trade groups right after lunch.

Payoffs to Writing Workshop in First Grade

Let's be honest, teaching Writer's Workshop is work! There is no manual to follow day after day or a black-line master to fill out. But to me, it is worth every bit of effort. This is real teaching, differentiated for this class and these students on this day. In keeping with district, state, and Common Core standards, *first graders get what they need when they need it.*

We see growth over time from writing every day. I look at a typical first grader like Alana, who writes "str i love you" in August, but by December can write a whole paragraph about a mouse:

Students make this growth because of Writing Workshop—focused mini-lessons, one-to-one conferencing, and lots of opportunities to write.

Writing gives first graders a feeling of accomplishment and builds their self esteem. Their work is valued by the teacher, classmates, the school community and their family. Donald Graves developed the five-stage writing process to immerse children in the real tasks of being a writer; children as young as five and six can feel like writers. Years ago, my school had an author visit by the amazing writer and illustrator, Jose Aruego (well known for illustrating *Leo the Late Bloomer*). We prepared for his visit by reading his books and examining the craft of the writing and illustrations. On the day he came, the excited first graders asked, "Can we take our books to the assembly to show him?" I loved it! They

Alana's writing the first day of school in August

Sister I love
you.

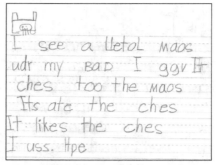

Writing growth of Alana by December

I see a little mouse
under my bed. I gave it
cheese too. The mouse
it ate the cheese.
It likes the cheese
I use. Happy.

Writing with voice!

I am good at
the tango. I'm
special because I like
my cats and I be
myself. I like home
work. I like to work.
I like reading.

felt ready to share with him, author to author. What a difference for emergent writers who years ago had to wait until their handwriting and spelling were perfected to get to write.

Teaching skills may sound boring and laborious. But in Writing Workshop, skills and strategies are taught, reinforced, and reviewed with pacing that provides satisfaction, requires less support and builds independence. I hope this book has given you dozens of ideas to use when they are right for your particular class.

With a little bit of effort and practice, your first graders will be able to make their voice heard through their writing. When my students write about a dying pet, I want to cry with them because their heart is on their sleeve. They also make me chuckle with surprise, like Marina did when she declared she is good at the tango!

Tango? Where did that come from? Because young writers choose their topics, their writing matters to them and the passion is almost palpable. (By the way, she demonstrated a tango after Author's Chair!)

I especially love the days when I remember to step back and just observe before rushing to the next writer. "Engagement" isn't an education buzz word when I see a group of students involved in their writing. They love the process that lets them express themselves every day with a new medium—the written word.

Every first grade teacher is working hard to teach reading, writing, spelling, grammar and punctuation. Writing Workshop links them all together. Reading and writing connects them as these reciprocal processes support each other. Reading wonderful books sparks children's imagination and gives ideas and models for writing. Best of all, the books we write and publish in first grade become another source of reading material in the classroom.

Yesenia chooses a student-authored book to read.

The Final Weeks of First Grade

First grade is almost done but there are ways to keep them writing until the last day of school.

WRITE AN AD

I ask the class to think about what kind of teacher they would like for Second Grade. I read out loud some job ads from the local newspaper. Using this as a model, the class writes an advertisement for next year's teacher. This is a lot of fun—and the second grade teachers enjoy reading them!

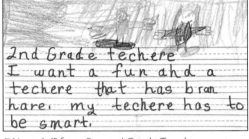

"Want Ad" for a Second Grade Teacher

INTRODUCE THEMSELVES

Our final letter of the year is written to their second grade teacher. They don't know whose class they will be in, so we make the salutation generic. We do no editing because I want their writing to speak for itself. We brainstorm some things to include:

Describe what they look like so their teacher will recognize them.

Tell what they are good at in school and other areas.

Tell what they will need help with next year in class.

Add interesting facts about themselves.

SUMMER WRITING IDEA FOR PARENTS

We have worked hard all year on writing, and I don't want the "Summer Slump" to create backsliders. We teachers always encourage summer reading, but what about summer writing? The last week of school I send a letter home to parents with ideas and suggestions for encouraging writing and even creating a writing center at home.

Reflections

Summer is here, and it is time for me to hug my students goodbye and let them reflect on first grade.

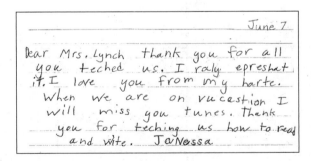

Hugs goodbye after a great year!

Dear Mrs. Lynch Thank you for all
you teached us. I really appreciate
it. I love you from my heart
When we are on vacation I
will miss you tons. Thank
you for teaching us how to read
and write. Janessa

ABC Chart

Aa	Bb	Cc	Dd	Ee
Ff	Gg	Hh	Ii	Jj
Kk	Ll	Mm	Nn	Oo
Pp	Qq	Rr	Ss	Tt
Uu	Vv	Ww	Xx	Yy
Zz				

Review Words to Start the Year

a	and	at	can
dad	have	he	I
in	is	it	like
love	mom	of	see
she	the	to	you

50 High-Frequency Words

Aa all and are	Bb because by	Cc can come	Dd did do	Ee each
Ff for friend from	Gg go	Hh have his her how here	Ii if into is	Jj
Kk know	Ll like little look love	Mm make may me more	Nn nice now	Oo or
Pp play	Qq	Rr	Ss said see she some	Tt the they this them
Uu	Vv	Ww who was what went when where	Xx	Yy Zz you

First Grade Writing Workshop © 2014 Judy Lynch • Scholastic Teaching Resources

100 High-Frequency Words

Aa	Bb	Cc	Dd	Ee
a as all at an and are	be because but by	came can come	dad day did do down	each eat

Ff	Gg	Hh	Ii	Jj
family find first for friend	get go good	had here has him have his he how her	I its if in is it	jump

Kk	Ll	Mm	Nn	Oo
know	like little look love	make my man may me mom	nice no not now	of out on over one or other

Pp	Qq	Rr	Ss	Tt
play put		read	said some saw see she so	than they that this the to them too then two

Uu	Vv	Ww	Xx	Yy Zz
up us	very	was when we where went who were will what with		you

Irregular High-Frequency Words

the	of	a	to
you	was	are	they
from	have	one	what
were	there	your	their
said	do	many	some
would	other	into	two
could	been	who	people
only	water	very	words
where	through	any	another
come	work	does	put
different	again	old	great
should	give	something	thought
both	often	together	world
want			

These irregular words represent 53 of the 200 most frequent words. Adapted from Dr. John Shefelbine.

Writing Workshop Record

Name	Mon.	Tues.	Wed.	Thur.	Fri.	Mon.	Tues.	Wed.	Thur.	Fri.

Mini-Lessons:

C = Conference   **C+** = Conference/student doing well   **C–** = Conference/concerns

P = Published   **?** = Student asked a question   ☆ = Student shared in Author's Chair

Name: _____

Date	Context	Anecdotal Notes	What does he/she know?	What does he/she need?

Title	Characters	Problem	Solution	Author's Message

Reproducible 8: Literature Comparison Chart

Content Conference Guide

Listen

- Look at the writer's face.
- Say, "Tell me about your writing."
- Suggest, "Read me the part you want help on."

   or

   "Read me the part you are proud of."

Tell Back

Restating what is written puts it clearly in the student's mind.

- Summarize what the student has read.
- Paraphrase it in your own words.

Ask Questions / Comment

- "I don't understand…"   (CLARIFY)
- "Tell me more about…"   (EXPAND)
- Who? What? When? Where? Why? How?   (DETAILS)
- "What do you plan next?"   (EXTEND)

Reflect

The lens a teacher uses when looking at writing:

- What does the student know?
- What does the student need?

Adapted from Donald Graves, Dublin Conference 1990

Paired-Writing Guide

WHO?

Emergent writers who need extra support to understand the writing process and how to get words down in print. Most young writers do not need this intensive 1:1 help.

WHEN?

During Writing Workshop while the student is attempting a rough draft. Volunteers and upper grade buddies can be trained to help in class with paired writing.

HOW?

1. Have a brief conversation to develop a sentence.
2. Student repeats the sentence to have it firmly in mind.
3. You may need to clap the words and count them.
4. Work word by word with the student:
   - Stretch word orally = "rubber-band writing"
     What do you hear first? What do you hear next?
   - Student records everything he/she can.
   - Teacher fills in the letters that are unfamiliar to the student to make an accurately spelled sentence.

     Take "to boxes" a few simple, phonetic words.

     Take "to fluency" a high-frequency word.

     Student rereads the entire sentence after each word is added.
5. Establish what the student will write next and leave him/her to work independently.

Do this only occasionally as needed.

Adapted from Helen Depree

Skills _____ Can Do as a Writer

1. _____

2. _____

3. _____

4. _____

5. _____

6. _____

7. _____

8. _____

9. _____

10. _____

11. _____

12. _____

13. _____

14. _____

15. _____

My Topics

Family	Friends	Animals

Sports	Games	Trips

Fiction/"Fake" Stories	All About Me	My Opinion/Other Ideas

Description: 5 Senses

What do you feel?

What do you taste?

What do you smell?

What do you hear?

What do you see?

Story Planning Graphic Organizer

Beginning

Characters   Looks   Acts

Setting

Problem

Middle

Event

Event

Event

Event

End

Solution

Simple Graphic Organizer
for Informational Writing

Topic

State a fact

State a fact

State a fact

Conclusion

Graphic Organizer for Informational Writing With Supporting Details

Topic

State a fact	Detail

State a fact	Detail

State a fact	Detail

Conclusion

First Grade Writing Workshop © 2014 Judy Lynch • Scholastic Teaching Resources

I Edit My Writing

Punctuation

. ☐   ? ☐   ! ☐

· ·

Capitals

I ☐

First word of sentence ☐

Names ☐

· ·

Spelling

☐

Making a Book Checklist

Check off when completed.

1. COVER
   Title, Author, Illustration ☐

2. TITLE PAGE ☐

3. DEDICATION PAGE ☐

4. RECOPY IN BEST WRITING ☐
   (If your teacher asks you to self-publish)

5. ILLUSTRATE TO MATCH STORY ☐

6. ABOUT THE AUTHOR ☐

7. STAPLE/BIND INTO A BOOK ☐

8. AUTHOR'S CHAIR ☐
   Practice reading 3 times to present your book.

Resources

Atwell, N. (1998). *In the middle: New understandings*. Portsmouth, NH: Heinemann.

Avery, C. (2002). *...And with a light touch, 2nd Edition*, Portsmouth, NH: Heinemann.

Beck, I. (2002). *Bringing words to life: Robust vocabulary instruction*. New York: Guilford Press.

Calkins, L. (1986, 1994). *The art of teaching writing*. Portsmouth, NH: Heinemann.

Cambourne, B., & Turbill, J. (1991). *Coping with chaos*. Portsmouth, NH: Heinemann.

Caplan, R. (1980). *Showing-writing: A training program to help students be specific*. Berkeley CA: University of California Press.

Caplan, R. (1984). *Writers in Training*, Lebanon, IN: Dale Seymour Publication.

Dorn, L. (2012). *Apprenticeship in literacy, 2nd ed.* Portland, ME: Stenhouse.

Graves, D. H. (1983). *Writing: Teachers and children at work*. Exeter, NH: Heinemann.

Graves, D. H. (1990). Writing Seminar in Dublin, Ireland (St. Patrick's College).

Haven, K. (2001). Wanted: A few good details—Writing details versus description. *The California Reader*, Winter 2001.

Moreton, D. & Berger, S. (1998). *Why write?* New York: Scholastic.

Oczkus, L. (2001). *Guided writing: Practical lessons, powerful results*. Portsmouth, NH: Heinemann.

Pulver, R. (2003). *Punctuation takes a vacation*. New York: Holiday House.

Tierney, R. J., & Shanahan, T. (1991). Research on the reading–writing relationship: Interactions, transactions, and outcomes. In R. Barr, M. L. Kamil, P. Mosenthal, & P. D. Pearson (Eds.), *Handbook of reading research* (Vol. 2, pp. 246-280). New York: Longman.

Turbill, J. (1995). *No better way to teach writing*. Portsmouth, NH: Heinemann.

Wood Ray, K. (2004). *About the authors: Writing workshop with our youngest writers*. Portsmouth, NH: Heinemann.